THE

Biblical Hebrew

COMPANION

FOR BIBLE SOFTWARE USERS

GRAMMATICAL TERMS
EXPLAINED FOR EXEGESIS

Michael Williams

ZONDERVAN®

ZONDERVAN

The Biblical Hebrew Companion for Bible Software Users
Copyright © 2015 Michael Williams

Requests for information should be addressed to:
Zondervan, 3900 *Sparks Dr. SE, Grand Rapids, Michigan 49546*

Library of Congress Cataloging-in-Publication Data

Williams, Michael James, 1956– author.
    Biblical Hebrew companion for Bible software users : grammatical terms explained
for exegesis / Michael Williams.
        pages cm
    Includes bibliographical references and index.
    ISBN 978-0-310-52130-3 (softcover)
    1. Hebrew language—Grammar. 2. Bible—Language, style. I. Title.
PJ4567.3.W55 2015
492.482'421—dc23   2015020796

Cover design: Faceout Studios
Cover photo: Shutterstock
Interior design: Kait Lamphere

Printed in the United States of America

16 17 18 19 20 21 22 23 24 25 · 20 19 18 17 16 15 14 13 12 11 10 9 8 7 6 5 4 3 2 1

TABLE OF CONTENTS

INTRODUCTION

Rationale and Purpose

The development of Bible software has facilitated access to the technical features of the original biblical languages for many more students of the sacred Scriptures. It was once the case that those who were interested in exploring the insights afforded by biblical Hebrew, for example, had to spend significant amounts of time and effort to learn that language's paradigms, vocabulary, grammar, and syntax. With the appearance of electronic resources that provide much of that information at the click of a mouse, the question legitimately arises whether the time and effort that characterized paleo-technological times is still warranted.

Unfortunately, individuals and academic institutions often settle on one of two extremes in responding to this question. One extreme insists on maintaining historical strategies for accessing the exegetical advantages of learning the details of the original languages. This is the "it was good enough for me in my day" approach. This approach is still effective, but ignores the potential benefits of the extraordinary technological advances that have occurred over the years. It is similar to insisting on the continued use of rotary telephones. Those still work too. But the purpose of the telephone—communication—has become realized to an almost inconceivably greater degree with smart phones. It is unjustifiable to ignore such technological advances or to refuse to utilize them in approaching the biblical text.

The opposite extreme position that individuals and academic institutions sometimes take is to mistakenly equate learning a Bible software program with learning the original biblical languages. A Bible software program may inform a person, for example, that a verb is an apocopated Hiphil Imperfect with a Waw Consecutive. While that information is certainly true, it is of absolutely no help to that person if they don't know what "apocopated," "Hiphil," "Imperfect," and "Waw Consecutive" look like, what they mean, or why anyone should care. Apart from such knowledge, simply knowing how to operate the Bible software program yields for the operator no benefit beyond that available to someone who has no knowledge at all of biblical languages.

What is needed for more fruitful Old Testament study, therefore, is a resource that occupies the vast and currently vacant middle ground between the traditional, full-blown academic study of biblical Hebrew on the one hand and complete ignorance of biblical Hebrew on the other. The purpose of this book is to helpfully occupy that middle ground.

Contents

Consequently, it is very important that the reader not confuse this resource with a grammar book. Introductory Hebrew grammar books abound, and several are listed at the end of this resource (See *Select Bibliography for Further Study*). While this resource does necessarily present some grammatical information (especially in the Appendices), its primary goal is to be a convenient tool for students of the Bible who seek to explore the text by means of biblical language software more deeply than a consideration of the English translation alone allows. But rather than simply leaving the software user with a pile of terminological detritus, this resource provides the reader with an explanation and demonstration of the terms the Bible software presents. Thus, the software user can productively use that information to enrich communal and personal study of the Bible.

In this way, this resource explains the "so what" aspect for the analytical grammatical terms encountered in the three leading Bible software programs: Accordance Bible Software, BibleWorks, Logos Bible Software, and Olive Tree. While these three main programs are the focus, this resource will also easily serve other Bible software programs and reference works. For each grammatical term these programs present, the user of this resource is provided three critical pieces of information: a description of what the grammatical feature looks like, an explanation of what the grammatical feature does, and an example of an exegetical insight into the biblical text afforded by an understanding of the grammatical feature that is not available or is not as clear in the English translations.

To make this resource even more user-friendly, the information described above for each grammatical term has been provided on two facing pages. This enables the user to see all the information for each term at once, without the need to turn a page.

Intended Users

This resource is designed to benefit anyone who owns a Bible software program that provides technical grammatical information about biblical Hebrew who would like to benefit more fully from that information. Such people include:

- Individuals who have never found the opportunity, resources, or inclination to learn the paradigms, vocabulary, grammar, and syntax of biblical Hebrew (or perhaps even these features in their own language), but would still like to benefit from the deeper insights into the biblical text that biblical Hebrew can provide.

- Pastors and other ministry leaders who may have learned and realized the benefits of knowing biblical Hebrew at one time but have experienced the loss of much of their language proficiency (with the resulting exegetical loss) because the time necessary to maintain it has been depleted by the demands of life and ministry.

- College and seminary students who are either: (1) engaged in a biblical Hebrew language course in which traditional language learning techniques are being employed, who could use this resource as a supplement that would provide them with simplified explanations and presentations of what they are learning, in addition to motivation for that learning by means of exegetical examples from actual biblical texts; or (2) no longer required to learn the biblical languages in their academic programs, thus closing off any exegetical fruit that understanding those biblical languages could provide for them and for those to whom they minister.

How to Use

This resource presumes ownership of or access to a biblical language software program. With the software program opened, placing the cursor over the Hebrew word should result in a grammatical analysis in a window somewhere on the screen. Each individual word of the grammatical analysis is treated separately in this resource. To find the information for each grammatical term, simply refer to the Table of Contents, where each term is conveniently listed in alphabetical order, along with alternative designations for that term that one may encounter in the various Bible software programs.

When you have located the grammatical term in this resource, you will find a description of its appearance (so you can recognize it in the Hebrew text), a brief description of the function of that grammatical feature, and an exegetical insight into a specific biblical text that demonstrates how a knowledge of the grammatical feature can clarify, enhance, deepen, or even correct what can be observed in English translations. Understanding how knowledge of a particular grammatical feature contributes toward exegesis in one passage will enable you to apply that knowledge fruitfully in analogous contexts.

Throughout the two-page discussions of grammatical features, and also throughout the discussions in the Appendices, any word in bold font indicates a separate treatment of that term in this resource.

Treatment of each term provided by the leading biblical software programs will, of course, not deal with significant features of Hebrew morphology, grammar, and syntax. For those whose appetite for such things will have been whetted, ultimate satisfaction can only be obtained by recourse to fuller grammatical treatments. Information regarding some of these has been provided at the end of this resource in a section entitled *Select Bibliography for Further Study*. However, as a sort of appetizer, and to explain some fundamental features of the Hebrew language (such as otherwise unexplained features of its appearance and pronunciation), several appendices have been provided at the end of this resource. These should equip the reader with everything necessary for a basic understanding of the form and sound of Hebrew words.

A *Scripture Index* has also been provided at the end of this resource to enable users to quickly locate Scripture passages discussed in the exegetical insights for the grammatical terms.

This resource enables anyone using biblical Hebrew language software to delve more deeply into the riches of the biblical text. There are amazing discoveries waiting to be unearthed in the Hebrew Bible. You now have all the tools you need to access them. Happy digging!

— ACKNOWLEDGMENTS —

In the course of teaching introductory biblical Hebrew at Calvin Theological Seminary for twenty years, both online and in residence in a variety of formats, I have benefitted from the questions and insights of countless students who have shouldered the burden of learning this language in which over two-thirds of the Bible is written. They continually and rightly press to understand the personal and ministerial payoff for their large investments of time, effort, and money. I owe a debt of gratitude to them for their many and varied contributions to this resource.

I also thank my colleagues, the administration, and the Board of Trustees of Calvin Seminary, who provided the opportunity and resources for me to work on this resource and encouraged me in its production.

Acknowledgment and appreciation also go to Zondervan, and particularly to Verlyn Verbrugge and Nancy Erickson, for recognizing the need for such a resource and assisting me with the mechanics of its realization.

Finally, my greatest thanks go to Dawn — my wife, coach, support, and closest friend. It hardly seems fair that she makes all the sacrifices and my name ends up on the book.

ABSOLUTE

What It Looks Like

The absolute form of a **noun** is best described by what it is not. It is the form of the noun when the noun is not in the **construct** form. In other words, it is the normal form of the noun, whether it is **masculine** or **feminine singular**, **plural**, or **dual**.

You can recognize that a noun is in its absolute form (or state) simply by looking for its normal endings and **vowel** patterns. (For these, see Noun later in this resource.) For example, here is the same masculine plural noun in both its absolute form and its construct form:

Absolute form   Construct form

The noun on the left has the normal דים ending of the masculine plural. This has changed to a י for the noun on the right. Because the noun on the left has the normal ending, it is the absolute form.

What It Does

As described later in this resource, the translation of the construct form of a noun will be followed by the word "of"; the absolute form of a noun will not. This will obviously have great significance for the relationship of nouns that occur together in a sentence. If the nouns are in the construct form, they will all be connected by the word "of." If the nouns are in the absolute form, they are simply describing the same thing with different terms. For example, consider the sentence:

"The daughter, the doctor, worked in the hospital."

In Hebrew, "the daughter" and "the doctor" would be two nouns in the absolute form describing the same person. Now consider the sentence:

"The daughter of the doctor worked in the hospital."

This sentence, though similar to the first, says something quite different. Now "the daughter" and "the doctor" are two different people. In Hebrew, "the daughter" would be in the construct form (because it is followed by "of") and "the doctor" would be in the absolute form.

An Exegetical Insight

The difference between an absolute noun and a construct noun can be seen by an examination of Numbers 25:2 in both the Hebrew and the English Bible. There we read that the Moabite women invited the Israelite men to "the sacrifices to their gods." In this verse we have two nouns, "the sacrifices" and "their gods." The important question we have to consider is how we are to understand the relationship of these two nouns to one another. If the two nouns were both in the absolute form, that would mean "the sacrifices" and "their gods" would be describing the same thing. In other words, the verse would be saying that the Moabites were making their gods their sacrifices; that is, their sacrifices *consisted* of their gods. This is a use of the word "of" in English that we find in such sentences as, "He ate a supper of grains of rice." But we notice in the Hebrew that the first noun is in the construct form, not the absolute. This enables us to see that the sacrifices the Moabites were making did not consist of their gods, but rather were those "of," or what they thought "belonged to," their gods. Such a critical difference rides on this single grammatical feature! In this case, the absolute form of the nouns would have signified a praiseworthy action (the destruction of their idols), while the construct form of the first noun unfortunately indicates exactly the opposite (condemnable idolatry). Too bad both nouns weren't in the absolute form!

ADJECTIVE

What It Looks Like

Hebrew adjectives can be difficult to recognize because they have the same endings as **noun**s. More specifically, adjectives have exactly the same endings as the nouns they are describing. The only exception to this is that adjectives have no **dual** ending like nouns do. Adjectives have only **singular** or **plural** endings. So, when an adjective is describing a dual noun, the adjective will have a plural ending.

If the adjective comes after the noun it is describing and agrees with the noun it is describing in gender, number, and definiteness/indefiniteness, then it is an attributive adjective (described more fully below).

If the adjective comes before or after the noun it is describing, does not have the **definite article**, but does agree with the noun it is describing in gender and number, then it is a predicative adjective (described more fully below).

If the adjective does not come before or after a noun, it is a substantive adjective (described more fully below).

What It Does

Adjectives describe things. In Hebrew they accomplish this in the same three ways they do in English:

- They can describe a noun without forming a sentence to do so. This kind of adjective is called an attributive adjective. For example, the word "free" in "the free people" describes (indicates an attribute of) the people but doesn't form a sentence in doing so. So, "free" in this case is an attribute adjective.

- They can describe a noun and form a sentence in doing so. This kind of adjective is called a predicative adjective because it forms a predication (or, a sentence). For example, the word "free" in "the people are free" describes the people and forms a sentence in doing so. So, "free" in this case is a predicative adjective. Notice how the adjective and the noun it is describing are separated by a form of the verb "to be" (in this case, "are"). This will always be the case with predicative adjectives.

- They can describe a noun by standing in place of the noun. This kind of adjective is called a substantive adjective because it acts like a noun (or substantive). For example, the word "free" in "the land of the free" is standing in place of "free people." So, "free" in this case is a substantive adjective.

An Exegetical Insight

Understanding what kind of adjective one is encountering in the text and the word it is describing can be very significant exegetically. For example, Psalm 19:9 in the English Bible (19:10 in Hebrew) says, "The fear of the Lord is pure, enduring forever" (יִרְאַת יְהוָה טְהוֹרָה עוֹמֶדֶת לָעַד). How do we know whether the adjective "pure" (טְהוֹרָה) is describing "fear" (יִרְאַת) or "the Lord" (יְהוָה)? In other words, is the verse asserting that the fear of the Lord is pure, or that the Lord himself is pure? Understanding how adjectives work can bring greater clarity here.

This psalm describes God's revelation in both creation (vv. 1–6) and in his word (vv. 7–11). This verse falls into the second section, which encourages believers to take confidence in the trustworthiness of God's revealed word. Of course God himself is pure and endures forever. But these adjectives can also describe his word, noted here as the "fear of the Lord" (that is, the means by which God has instructed his people in how to live with appropriate reverence, or fear, in his presence). The "Lord" is grammatically **masculine**. But the adjective "pure" has a **feminine** ending, as does the word "fear." Because of this agreement, we can see that the psalmist is describing here the perfect character, or purity, of God's word (the "fear of the Lord") — another reason for us to trust it completely.

ADVERB

What It Looks Like

A Hebrew adverb has no distinguishing features that enable us to differentiate it from other kinds of words. It has no markers for **person**, gender, or number. One must either learn adverbs individually or depend on Bible software or other Hebrew language resources for their identification. The number of pure adverbs in Hebrew is limited. Hebrew often communicates an adverbial sense through other means. These include:

- Co-opted **noun**s, such as יַחַד "together"
- Co-opted **adjective**s (especially in the **feminine** form), such as רִאשׁוֹנָה "formerly" (רִאשׁוֹן is an adjective meaning "first.")
- Co-opted **Infinitive Absolutes** (especially in the **Hiphil stem**), such as הַרְבֵּה "much"
- Co-opted **pronoun**s, such as זֶה "here" (As a pronoun זֶה means "this.")
- Co-opted **number**s, such as אַחַת "once" (As a number אַחַת means "one.")
- **Preposition**s attached to nouns, such as בִּמְאֹד "very" (מְאֹד means "strength.")
- Certain **suffix**es attached to nouns or adjectives, such as יוֹמָם "by day" (יוֹם means "day.")

What It Does

A Hebrew adverb performs the same functions as an English adverb; that is, it may modify a **verb**, adjective, or another adverb. An adverb can tell us "how" (He studied *eagerly*), "when" (He studied *daily*), "where" (He studied *here*), or "how much" (He studied *inadequately*).

An Exegetical Insight

As with other kinds of Hebrew words, there is often more than one possible meaning for an adverb. The context must dictate which meaning the author intends. There are times, however, when more than one possible meaning would fit the context. Such a situation makes things difficult for a translator, who must choose only one meaning for the English translation. But the person who can access the Hebrew text can be made aware of the other possibilities, and these other possibilities can yield a deeper understanding of what is being communicated.

One instance of an adverb that may be translated in two possible ways is found in Psalm 37:8. The second half of this verse is usually translated: "do not fret — it leads only to evil" (אַל־תִּתְחַר אַךְ־לְהָרֵעַ). The next-to-last word (אַךְ) is an adverb that has two meanings that may apply in this context. It can have a restrictive sense, meaning "nothing but." This meaning is captured in the English translation above as "only." But "only" in English has multiple possible meanings. In addition to "nothing but," it could also mean, for example, "especially" (I *only* did this for you), "merely" (It's *only* a scratch), or several other possibilities.

The intended sense of "only" in Psalm 37:8 is clarified when we consider another possible meaning of the word. Biblical language software informs us that the Hebrew adverb אַךְ can also have an emphasizing sense, meaning "surely." A possible translation of the second half of Psalm 37:8 with this sense would be: "do not fret — it surely leads to evil." This other possible translation clarifies the sense of "only" in the English translation. The sense of "only" in this context is communicating certainty. If fretting leads to *nothing but* trouble, then fretting *surely* results in trouble. Being able to access the meanings of this Hebrew adverb did not result in a different understanding than that provided by the English translation, but it did result in a clarified understanding.

APOCOPATED

What It Looks Like

An apocopated **verb** looks like an **Imperfect** verb that has been shortened. In fact, the verb "apocopate" simply means "to cut off." So, an apocopated verb is one that has been "cut off" or "shortened." The only kind of verb that is susceptible to this shortening is one whose third **root consonant** is a ה. The shortening (or apocopation) occurs for only two reasons: (1) when a **Waw Consecutive** is attached to the front of the verb; or (2) when the verb is a **Jussive**. The shortening will result in the loss of the ה of the root (that is, the verb's last root consonant). Usually there is some resulting change in the remaining **vowel**s as well, but the exact pattern varies.

For example, consider the verb בנה "to build":

| Normal Imperfect | Imperfect + Waw Consecutive | Jussive |

You can see that the ending of the normal Imperfect verb (ה ֶ) has been cut off (apocopated) for the Imperfect with a Waw Consecutive and for the Jussive. The shortening for these two forms is exactly the same. The only difference, of course, is that the Imperfect with a Waw Consecutive has the Waw Consecutive attached to the front of the verb. Another difference that may *sometimes* occur is that the Jussive form *may* be followed by the **particle** נָא־ (which is not translated).

What It Does

The apocopated, or shortened, form simply lets you know that you have encountered either an Imperfect with a Waw Consecutive or a Jussive of a three-consonant verb whose third consonant is a ה. For the appearance and function of the Imperfect, the Waw Consecutive, and the Jussive, see the appropriate entries in this resource.

An Exegetical Insight

Because apocopation signals only one of two options (a Jussive or an Imperfect with a Waw Consecutive attached), the presence or absence of a Waw Consecutive will enable one to determine which option is correct in a given context.

Consider, for example, Genesis 1:3. There we encounter the Bible's first apocopated form: יְהִי. This is apocopated from the normal Imperfect form יִהְיֶה (from the three-consonant root היה "to be"). If one didn't recognize that this verb form is apocopated, one would translate this verb with its normal Imperfect sense: "And God said, 'There will be light.'" But this translation presents God as no more than an informed onlooker. He appears as one who knows what will happen but has no role in bringing it about. However, once we recognize that יְהִי is an apocopated form, we still need to determine whether it is a Jussive or an Imperfect with a Waw Consecutive attached. Since there is no Waw Consecutive attached to the front of this verb, it must be a Jussive—a command form. So we should translate this sentence as "And God said, 'Let there be light!'"

Simply recognizing the apocopated form has resulted in a profound change in how one perceives God in this verse. Rather than being a detached, uninvolved onlooker who merely reports what will happen, he is instead revealed as the very one who is commanding light to come into existence. Even apocopated forms can bring glory to God!

—— COHORTATIVE ——

What It Looks Like

A Cohortative **verb** can be recognized by the simultaneous presence of two distinctive features:

- It will have either an **Alef** (א) or a **Nun** (נ) coming before the three-**consonant root** of the verb.
- It will usually have a **Qamets He** (הָ) coming after the three-consonant root of the verb.

Note the presence of these two features in the following example of a Cohortative form of the root שׁמר:

הָ at the end   א at the front

What It Does

The Cohortative is a volitional **conjugation**. That means it communicates something about the will (or volition) of the speaker. The Cohortative, by means of its distinctive forms, indicates a wish, resolve, or command.

For example, the form above (אֶשְׁמְרָה) comes from the root שׁמר, meaning "to guard." The א at the beginning signals the first **person singular** ("I"), as it does in the **Imperfect conjugation**. But when this feature appears in combination with the הָ at the end, one can recognize that this verb form is a Cohortative. So this verb must be translated in a way that expresses the will of the speaker. The specific way the will of the speaker is communicated in an English translation is, of course, ultimately dependent upon the context.

An Exegetical Insight

Consider Psalm 13 in both the Hebrew and English. This psalm is a lament. The psalmist is lamenting that God seems to have forgotten him. The psalmist is wrestling with his own negative thoughts and that his enemies seem to be triumphing over him. But then in the last verse in English (the second half of the last verse in Hebrew) we encounter the Cohortative form אָשִׁירָה. The English translation simply renders this as "I will sing" (the Lord's praise). But recognizing this form as a Hebrew Cohortative enables us to understand this sentence at a much deeper level.

The Cohortative signals an assertion of the speaker's will. And it is certainly going to take an assertion of the will on the psalmist's part to sing the Lord's praises when everything seems to be going wrong all around him. Yet this is exactly what he is committing himself to do. This is no "easy-believism" or recourse to a hypocritical expression of happiness. The psalmist certainly knows who God is and what God has already done for him. But the psalmist does not like or understand what is going on in his life, and would dearly love for things to be different. Nevertheless, in confident trust in God's "unfailing love," the psalmist commits himself to giving God the praise that is God's due. It is as though the psalmist is saying, "No matter how bad things get, no person or circumstance is going to stop me from singing the praises of the Lord!"

The appearance of the Cohortative at this critical juncture of faith and negative circumstances gives us some insight into the psalmist's faith by enabling us to recognize this wonderful assertion of his will. It also invites us to similarly assert our own will to praise.

──── COMMON ────

What It Looks Like

"Common" **pronoun**s:

- אָנֹכִי or אֲנִי (meaning "I")
- אֲנַחְנוּ or נַחְנוּ (meaning "we")

"Common" pronoun (pronominal) **suffix**es:

- יְ (meaning "my") attached to the end of many kinds of words
- יְ (meaning "my") attached to the end of **plural noun**s and four **preposition**s (אֶל, עַל, תַּחַת, and אַחַר)
- נוּ (meaning "our") attached to the end of many kinds of words

Consonants at the beginning of a **verb** that indicate "common":

- א (meaning "I")
- נ (meaning "we")

Endings on a verb that indicate "common":

- יְ (meaning "I" or "my")
- נוּ (meaning "we" or "our")

The common **demonstrative adjective**: אֵלֶּה (meaning "these")

What It Does

Hebrew grammatical forms that have gender usually indicate that grammatical gender by the way they are written. These gendered forms are either **masculine** or **feminine**; Hebrew has no neuter. However, some kinds of words (see above) that have gender indicated in most of their forms may also have forms that do not specify gender. The term "common" designates these forms. For example, "I" in English and Hebrew does not specify the gender of the person indicated. So, in both English and Hebrew, this pronoun would be designated as "common" — that is, as grammatically neither specifically masculine nor feminine.

An Exegetical Insight

In English, the pronoun "you" could be **singular** or plural, masculine or feminine. One couldn't find a more "common" pronoun. When this word appears in English translations, therefore, the reader might be left a bit confused regarding exactly who is being specified. Consider, for example, Zechariah 9:10–11:

> [10]I will take away the chariots from Ephraim
> and the warhorses from Jerusalem,
> and the battle bow will be broken.
> He will proclaim peace to the nations.
> His rule will extend from sea to sea
> and from the River to the ends of the earth.
> [11]As for you, because of the blood of my covenant with you,
> I will free your prisoners from the waterless pit.

The referent of the "you" mentioned at the beginning of verse 11 is a bit confusing. Is it "the nations" or "the ends of the earth"? Is it Zechariah or some other individual? Here the clouds of confusion dissipate when we learn that in Hebrew, unlike in English, "you" is not a "common" pronoun. In this passage, the Hebrew word for "you" is grammatically feminine and singular. So we look backward for its feminine singular referent and find it in verse 9: "Daughter Zion" or "Daughter Jerusalem."

Prophecy is already difficult to understand. "Common" grammatical forms can make our understanding even more difficult. Thankfully, Hebrew has far fewer common forms than English and so provides us with that much more clarity.

CONJUGATION

What It Looks Like

There are eight conjugations in biblical Hebrew: **Perfect, Imperfect, Cohortative, Imperative, Jussive, Infinitive Construct, Infinitive Absolute**, and **Participle**. See the entries in this resource for the specific appearance of each one of these. In general, however, each conjugation is recognized by what it adds to the three-**consonant root**. It may add consonants and **vowels** to the *end* of the root or to the *front* of the root. The conjugation may also be recognized by what it adds *within* the three-consonant root.

Consider, for example the three-consonant root שׁמר. Among the various changes apparent in the form שָׁמַרְתָּ, we notice that a תָּ has been added to the *end*. The location of this addition enables us to recognize this form as an example of the **Perfect** conjugation. Alternatively, consider the form תִּשְׁמֹר. It has added a תִּ to the *front* of the three-consonant root שׁמר. The location of this addition enables us to recognize this form as an example of the Imperfect conjugation. Finally, consider the form שֹׁמֵר. It has added a specific vowel pattern *within* the three-consonant root שׁמר. This pattern enables us to recognize this form as an example of the Participle conjugation. Each verb stem will have its own unique elements that it adds to the front, end, or within the three-consonant root in order to form its various conjugations.

What It Does

Each conjugation specifies a particular kind of verbal idea. So, recognizing the conjugation enables us to understand the kind of verbal idea intended by the author. That kind of verbal idea could be incomplete action or completed action. It could be a command or an emphasis. It could be ongoing or incipient action. It could be one of several other kinds of verbal ideas as well. Recognizing the particular conjugation enables us to understand more precisely what the author means in a given text.

An Exegetical Insight

Psalm 1:6 begins with a wonderful assurance that "the LORD watches over the way of the righteous." But the English verbal idea, "watches over," could be understood in a variety of ways. It could be understood to mean "*occasionally* watches over," as in "The man watches over the oil level in his car." That is, he doesn't do it all the time, but rather somewhat regularly. He checks it every now and then. "Watches over" could also be understood to mean "watches over *whenever necessary*," as in "He watches what he eats." Because he is not always eating, he does not always have to be watching. Or, "watches over" could even be understood to mean *whenever*, without any implication of how often, as in "Who in your family watches over the finances?" That is, whenever someone gets around to giving some attention to your family's financial matters (daily, weekly, monthly), who does it?

But the conjugation (participle) of the verbal form in this part of Psalm 1:6 clarifies what the author intends. The conjugation in this verse indicates a continuing action, an action that is in progress. So we can state with confidence that the LORD does not just "watch over" the lives of the righteous at times or when they get into jams or whenever he gets around to it. No, he does so continuously, uninterruptedly. The psalmist is expressing his confidence in that fact that the lives of God's people are always under his attentive watch and care. That's why, as verse 1 asserts, those people are "blessed"! In this verse, understanding the significance of the conjugation has led to a deeper level of confidence and security in ongoing divine care that is not available in the English translation alone.

CONJUNCTION

What It Looks Like

The biblical Hebrew conjunction *always* attaches directly to the front of a word. It doesn't exist independently. You will encounter several different forms of the conjunction in biblical Hebrew. The exact form depends on the **consonant**s and **vowel**s that are present at the beginning of the word to which the conjunction is attached. Here are all the variations of the form you may encounter, shown attached to a word ([   ]):

As you can see from the above forms, *all* the varieties of the conjunction include a **Waw** (ו). In fact, with only very rare exceptions, *every time* you see a word in Hebrew beginning with a Waw, you know you have encountered a conjunction. It is therefore relatively easy to recognize.

What It Does

The Hebrew conjunction performs the same function as English conjunctions. It links words, phrases, or sentences. The one Hebrew conjunction can be translated with a variety of English conjunctions: "and," "also," "even," "but," "or," "for," "nor," "then," "so," "now," "while," etc. The particular word used to translate the conjunction in any given passage depends entirely on the context.

An Exegetical Insight

As you can see, the Hebrew conjunction has many possible legitimate translation possibilities. This wealth of possibilities can become problematic in some contexts. Translating with one possible English word can mean something significantly different than translating with another possible English word. Translations must necessarily choose only one of the available options. This obscures other real possibilities from the English reader.

For example, consider the well-known verses, Genesis 1:1 – 2:

[1]In the beginning God created the heavens and the earth.
[2]Now the earth was formless and empty....

If you look carefully at the Hebrew text of this passage, you'll see that the word translated as "Now" at the beginning of verse 2 is the conjunction (וְ). Just consider how this passage might be understood differently if the conjunction were translated with one of its other possible meanings:

- *But* the earth was formless and empty....

  This translation suggests that because God created the earth, we might expect it to be perfect from the start of its existence, *instead of* chaotic and devoid of life.

- *While* the earth was formless and empty....

  This translation suggests that God's creative activity took place *while* the earth was formless and empty; that is, the earth was *already* here.

- *Or* the earth was formless and empty....

  This translation suggests that one of two situations existed. *Either* God created the earth, *or* the earth was formless and empty.

We could obviously multiply examples, but you get the point. How this little conjunction is translated can have huge implications for our understanding of what is going on in the text. It is helpful to know the range of possibilities with which the English translations are wrestling so that you understand the differences between them, as well as the possible theological implications of those differences.

CONSTRUCT

What It Looks Like

Nouns in the construct form (or state) can often be identified by their appearance.

- **Masculine plural** construct forms usually end in ‏ְי‎. See, for example, the difference between the normal (or **absolute**) masculine plural form of the noun ‏דָּבָר‎ and its masculine plural construct form:

Absolute form	Construct form

The noun on the left has the normal ‏ִים‎ ending of the masculine plural noun. This has changed to a ‏ְי‎ for the noun on the right. Because the noun on the right has the ‏ְי‎ ending, it is the construct form.

- **Feminine singular** construct forms usually end in ‏ַת‎. See, for example, the difference between the normal (or absolute) feminine singular form of the noun ‏תּוֹרָה‎ and its feminine singular construct form:

Absolute form	Construct form

The noun on the left has the normal ‏ָה‎ ending of the feminine singular noun. This has changed to a ‏ַת‎ for the noun on the right. Because the noun on the right has the ‏ַת‎ ending, it is the construct form.

- The construct forms of masculine singular and feminine plural nouns can be recognized not by their endings, but because their internal **vowel**s are often different than those of their non-construct, or absolute, forms. See Noun in this guide for the non-construct forms of masculine singular and feminine plural nouns.

What It Does

The construct form of a word is the Hebrew way of saying that the word is followed by "of" and then another noun. For example, the masculine plural construct form of דִּבְרֵי) דָּבָר, meaning "words") followed by the absolute noun סֵפֶר (meaning "book") would mean "words *of* a book" (דִּבְרֵי סֵפֶר). The words linked by "of" are said to be in a construct chain. The definiteness or indefiniteness (see **Definite Article**) of the very last noun of this chain determines the definiteness or the indefiniteness of all the nouns in the chain. In the example above, the last noun in the chain is indefinite ("*a* book"). That means the noun linked to it by "of" is also indefinite ("words" instead of "*the* words").

An Exegetical Insight

The construct form of the noun indicates that the translation of the word should be followed by "of." But the word "of" is as vague in Hebrew as it is in English. One of the titles for the Messiah given in Isaiah 9:6 (9:5 in Hebrew) is "Prince of Peace" (שַׂר־שָׁלוֹם). To understand the richness of this expression, we have to consider all the possible ways "of" can be understood in Hebrew. "Of" can mean:

- *consisting of*, as in "the tablets *of* stone" (לוּחֹת הָאֲבָנִים, Deut 9:10)
- *containing*, as in "the ark *of* the covenant" (אֲרוֹן הָעֵדוּת, Exod 26:33)
- *sphere of influence*, as in "the king *of* Israel" (מֶלֶךְ יִשְׂרָאֵל, 1 Sam 26:20)
- *belonging to*, as in "the sword *of* Goliath" (חֶרֶב גָּלְיָת, 1 Sam 22:10)
- *characterized by*, as in "the mountain *of* holiness" (הַר הַקֹּדֶשׁ, Zech 8:3)

Other possibilities exist as well. So, which meaning applies for the "Prince of Peace"? Perhaps more than one. Contemplating the richness of possibilities enables us to ponder this messianic title more deeply.

—— DEFINITE ARTICLE ——
(Article)

What It Looks Like

The Hebrew definite article normally consists of three parts: the **consonant** He, the **vowel** Patakh, and a **Dagesh** (a dot) in the first consonant of the **noun** or **adjective** to which the article is attached. Here is how the noun מֶלֶךְ ("king") looks with and without the definite article:

a king   the king

The two words are identical except for the He, Patakh, and Dagesh that have been attached directly to the front of the word on the right.

When the first consonant of the word to which the definite article is attached is an א, ה, ח, ע, or ר, the definite article may look a bit different because these five consonants cannot have a Dagesh inside them. Consequently, when the definite article is attached to words beginning with one of these consonants, the vowel under the ה of the definite article may change to a **Qamets** or a **Segol**. For example, note the forms of the definite article attached to the nouns עִיר, "city," and עָפָר, "dust":

Note that the usual form of the definite article · הַ has changed to הָ (for "the city") and הֶ (for "the dust") because the first consonant of the nouns to which it is attached (ע) is unable to take a Dagesh.

What It Does

The definite article simply makes the word to which it is attached *definite*. That means the word is now made specific or differentiated from all similar nouns. In English we indicate this specificity by using the word "the" (note the first example above). Note that unlike English, Hebrew has no *indefinite* article ("a" or "an").

An Exegetical Insight

In 2 Samuel 12, the prophet Nathan recounts to King David a story about a rich man with many possessions who took from a poor man the only thing that man owned and loved. David didn't know that Nathan was describing in parable form what David had just done by taking Uriah's wife, Bathsheba, for himself. After Nathan ends his story, David expresses outrage that anyone could carry out such a selfish, unfeeling act and declares that the man who has done such a thing should die. In verse 7, Nathan then drives home the point of his parable by saying to King David: "You are the man!"

The words translated in English as "the man" represent the Hebrew הָאִישׁ. Note the presence of the definite article (here written as הָ) attached to the front of the noun אִישׁ, "man." On this single grammatical feature hangs the whole force of the narrative. There would be no point at all to Nathan's prophetic judgment speech if he had only said to David, "You are *a* man." This would only be stating the obvious. But by using the definite article, Nathan has driven home his point that David is not just *any* man. No, Nathan is accusing David of being the specific man Nathan has just been describing in his parable — *the* man David himself has rightly condemned. In this verse, there is a life-and-death difference between *a* and *the*. All of David's indignation and ultimate self-condemnation ride upon the back of the definite article.

DEFINITE DIRECT OBJECT MARKER

(Direct Object Marker, Untranslatable Mark of the Accusative Case, Object, Direct Object)

What It Looks Like

The definite direct object marker has a few possible forms, with no difference in meaning between them:

$$אֵת \quad \text{or} \quad ־אֶת \quad \text{or} \quad ־את$$

The form on the left occurs independently. The form in the middle is always attached to a following word (the definite direct object) with a Maqqef (a raised connecting line). The form on the right occurs with **pronoun suffix**es that begin with a vowel. (For these, see the entry in this resource entitled Pronoun, Suffix.)

What It Does

The definite direct object marker has no translation value of its own. It simply exists for one purpose—to indicate the direct object in a sentence, when that direct object is definite. The direct object in a sentence is the word that directly receives the action of the **verb**. For example, consider the sentence, "I kicked the can." In this sentence the verb is "kicked." "The can" is directly receiving the action of the verb, so it is the direct object. In this example, the direct object is also definite (preceded by the **definite article** "the"). Therefore, in Hebrew, this direct object would be preceded by the definite direct object marker. In the sentence, "I kicked *a* can," the direct object is indefinite. In Hebrew, therefore, "a can" would *not* be preceded by the definite direct object marker.

An Exegetical Insight

In English, the subject of the verb regularly comes before the verb and the direct object follows the verb. So, in the sentence "Bill hit John," we know that Bill is the subject and poor John is the direct object receiving the unwelcome action. In Hebrew, however, the verb regularly comes first in a sentence. We can usually recognize the subject by its agreement with the verb in gender and number (See Verb in this resource). But we have a potential problem when the subject *and* the direct object are both the same gender and number as the verb. Then it can be difficult to discern who is doing what to whom. Here is where the definite direct object marker sheds light on our path.

For example, in Genesis 6–7 God sends a flood to "wipe from the face of the earth the human race" (6:7). In his great mercy, God does not completely destroy everyone, though only a few remain: "Only Noah was left, and those with him in the ark" (7:23). In Genesis 8:1, we're told with only a few words what evidently causes the floodwaters finally to subside: וַיִּזְכֹּר אֱלֹהִים אֶת־נֹחַ ("But God remembered Noah"). The last word in this sentence נֹחַ (Noah) is preceded by the definite direct object marker אֶת־, informing us that it is Noah who is on the receiving end of God's gracious remembering. Without this particle, the grammar alone could allow one to conclude wrongly that Noah is the subject of the sentence (that is, "Noah remembered God"), and so it is *his* remembering God that motivates God to act on his behalf. An important theological issue is at stake. The little definite direct object marker has prevented us from potentially mistakenly concluding that Noah has somehow earned God's saving action and has instead kept our focus where it belongs—on God's unmerited mercy on mankind.

DEMONSTRATIVE ADJECTIVE

What It Looks Like

Like all **adjective**s, there are **masculine** and **feminine**, **singular** and **plural** forms of the demonstrative adjective. These forms are provided below:

NEAR DEMONSTRATIVE ADJECTIVES	
MASCULINE SINGULAR ("this")	זֶה
FEMININE SINGULAR ("this")	זֹאת
COMMON PLURAL ("these")	אֵלֶּה

FAR DEMONSTRATIVE ADJECTIVES	
MASCULINE SINGULAR ("that")	הוּא
FEMININE SINGULAR ("that")	הִיא
MASCULINE PLURAL ("those")	הֵמָּה or הֵם
FEMININE PLURAL ("those")	הֵנָּה or הֵן

What It Does

Like all adjectives, the demonstrative adjectives describe a person, place, or thing. The demonstrative adjective is called that simply because one must *demonstrate* when one says it. When I say, for example, "*this* book," people will look to see what book I am indicating—perhaps even indicating by pointing. The demonstrative adjectives that suggest I'm indicating something far away are called "far" demonstrative adjectives. Conversely, those that suggest I'm indicating something nearby are called "near" demonstrative adjectives. Demonstrative adjectives make the **noun**s they're describing specific and definite. I don't mean *any* book when I say "this book" or "that book"; I mean a specific one.

When the third-person, demonstrative adjectives are used substantively, they are effectively **pronoun**s. That's because there is no difference in meaning between saying "he," for example, and *that* [masculine singular] one."

An Exegetical Insight

In Exodus 32, the people of Israel have grown impatient with Moses' absence while he is on the mountain conversing with God. So, they direct Aaron to make for them other gods. Overly compliant, Aaron has the people give him their gold earrings from which he forms an "idol cast into the shape of a calf" (32:4). When the people see the idol, they say, "*These* are your gods, Israel, who brought you up out of Egypt" (32:4).

Notice how the people use the *near* demonstrative, "these." They mistakenly believe God is distant from them. They haven't seen his representative for a while and they assume that God is just as far removed from them as Moses. So they attempt to make for themselves a replacement for God, a god who could be near to them. Their fundamental theological error is reflected in the demonstrative adjective they use. They don't realize that God is both transcendent (far) *and* immanent (near). Moses would later remind the people that there is no other nation whose gods are near to them the way that Israel's God is near to them (Deut 4:7).

God responds to his people's disobedience by telling Moses, "I have seen *these* people, . . . and they are a stiff-necked people." Israel's use of the near demonstrative to describe their idol reflected their wrong understanding of God. God's use of the near demonstrative to describe Israel reflects his perfect understanding of his people.

DIRECTIONAL HE ENDING

(Directive ה, Locative ה)

What It Looks Like

The directional He ending consists of an *unaccented* Qamets He (הָ) attached to the end of a word:

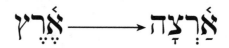

As is apparent in the above example, when the directional He ending is attached to the word, the **vowels** of the word itself may consequently be slightly altered, but this change of vowels does not affect the meaning of the word.

What It Does

The directional He ending indicates motion toward the **noun** to which it is attached. In English we sometimes do this by attaching the suffix "-ward" to a noun. For example, in the sentence, "the malfunctioning satellite plummeted earthward," the "-ward" ending on "earth" accomplishes exactly the same function as the Hebrew directional He ending. Of course, motion toward something may also be indicated in other ways in Hebrew. The most common way is by means of the **preposition** אֶל. There is no difference in meaning between the use of this preposition and the use of the directional He ending, just as there is no difference in English between the sentences "The malfunctioning satellite plummeted earthward" and "The malfunctioning satellite plummeted toward earth." In both cases the prospects for the satellite's future do not look good.

An Exegetical Insight

In Genesis 37 Joseph has two dreams that reveal something of his future. In verses 5–11 he recounts these dreams to his brothers and his father. The first dream involves sheaves of grain, representing his brothers, bowing down to him. The second dream expands on the first. It involves "the sun and moon and eleven stars," representing his entire family, bowing down to him. Unsurprisingly, Joseph's brothers and father don't receive this report positively. But their less than enthusiastic reactions spring from very different emotions. Joseph's brothers are jealous of Joseph (37:11), and his dreams only fuel their hatred of him (37:8). Joseph's father, Jacob, also has a negative reaction to Joseph's dreams, but it is not one that arises from jealousy or hatred. Instead, Jacob's reaction springs from amazement.

Jacob's amazement results from his understanding of the implications of what Joseph is telling him. Jacob is aware that Joseph's dreams imply the reversal of ancient Near Eastern norms in which younger sons are at the bottom of the family pecking order. Joseph's dreams suggest exactly the opposite of this norm. Not only would Joseph eclipse all of his older brothers in importance, but he would even rise above his own parents in importance. Jacob highlights this directional shift by adding a significant detail—the directional He ending—to his question to Joseph: "Will your mother and I and your brothers actually come and bow down *to the ground* [אַרְצָה] before you?" (37:10, italics added). "To the ground" does not occur in Joseph's account of his dreams (37:9). By the addition of this detail, Jacob reveals that he is aware that a significant directional shift in the course of God's plans for his chosen line has been signaled by these iconoclastic dreams of Joseph. The future of Jacob's entire family will rest on what subsequently happens to Joseph.

DUAL

What It Looks Like

The dual is indicated by a special ending attached only to **nouns**. For **absolute** nouns, the dual ending is ـַיִם. See, for example, the singular and dual forms of יָד, "hand":

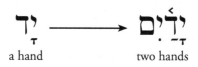

| a hand | two hands |

When the dual ending is attached to **feminine singular** nouns ending in הָ, the ה of the feminine singular ending turns to a ת, and then the dual ending is added:

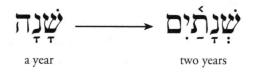

| a year | two years |

The dual ending for **construct** nouns is ـֵי:

| two hands | two hands *of* |

What It Does

As can be seen in the examples above, the dual ending simply indicates there are two of whatever noun it is attached to. Not all nouns may take a dual ending. Dual endings will be found on nouns denoting things that naturally occur in pairs (such as body parts) and some expressions of time ("two years," for example) and number ("two times," for example).

An Exegetical Insight

Joseph was no doubt confused. His dreams suggested that he would rise to a position of prominence in his family. But he had been sold into slavery by his own brothers. Then he had been falsely accused of a crime for which he had been imprisoned. Now, because he had been able to interpret Pharaoh's dreams when no one else could, he had been raised to the number two position in Egypt, second only to Pharaoh himself. The confusion Joseph experienced as a consequence of these perplexing events is reflected in the names he gives to the two sons born to him in Egypt. The name of the first son is Manasseh, meaning "cause to forget." In Genesis 41:51, Joseph admits, "God has *made me forget* all my trouble and all my father's household" (italics added)—which is a strange thing to say if he really believed that his dreams would be fulfilled. In 41:52, Joseph names his second son Ephraim (אֶפְרַיִם), which is related to the Hebrew word for "fruit" (פְּרִי). One can see that the Hebrew form of this name has a dual ending. The dual ending on the name of this second son is Joseph's way of saying that not only has God made Joseph fruitful by giving him one son, God has made Joseph *twice* fruitful by giving him *two* sons. Joseph's double fruitfulness is again referred to by his father in Genesis 49:22 (italics added):

> Joseph is a *fruitful* vine,
> > a *fruitful* vine near a spring,
> > whose branches climb over a wall.

Contrary to Joseph's assertion that God had made him forget his father's household, it is precisely Joseph's father, Jacob, whom God uses to bless Joseph with double fruitfulness—a double fruitfulness foreshadowed by the name of Joseph's own son, Ephraim (אֶפְרַיִם).

ENERGIC NUN

(Nun energicum)

What It Looks Like

The energic Nun is the name given to the Nun that occasionally appears between the **verb stem** and any **pronoun/pronominal suffix**. The energic Nun may appear as the regular **consonant** Nun (נ) or, more commonly, will assimilate into the following consonant. The energic Nun usually occurs with verbs in the **Imperfect conjugation**, rarely with verbs in the **Perfect** conjugation. The following two examples illustrate the energic Nun in both its unassimilated and assimilated forms.

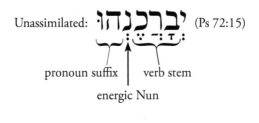

Unassimilated: יְבָרֲכֶנְהוּ (Ps 72:15)

pronoun suffix | verb stem

energic Nun

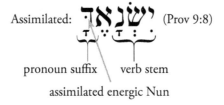

Assimilated: יִשְׂנָאֶךָ (Prov 9:8)

pronoun suffix \ verb stem

assimilated energic Nun

What It Does

Although its precise function in Hebrew is debated, traditionally it has been thought that the energic Nun gives the verb form to which it is attached additional strength, emphasis, or *energy*.

An Exegetical Insight

The Hebrew Scriptures inform us that from among all the nations, God singled out a surprisingly unremarkable one to be his special people. Yet, in spite of their unexceptional character, God had determined that they would be the ones with whom he would enter into a covenant relationship. They would receive his focused attention and care. In verse 10 of the song of Moses recorded in Deuteronomy 32, Moses celebrates God's special emphasis on Israel:

> He shielded him [that is, Israel] (יְסֹבְבֶנְהוּ) and cared for him (יְבוֹנְנֵהוּ);
> he guarded him (יִצְּרֶנְהוּ) as the apple of his eye.

Notice that all of the verbs have an energic Nun before the 3ms pronoun suffix הוּ.

While it is dangerous to build exegetical conclusions on grammatical features that are not fully understood, if the traditional understanding of the significance of the energic Nun is correct, we may wonder whether Moses is using this grammatical construction to remind God's chosen people of their uniquely favored status. By using verbs that contain the energic Nun, Moses may be highlighting God's loving, attentive, concerted efforts to nurture and safeguard his chosen people.

Moses subsequently goes on in this song to lament the fact that this devoted fatherly attention on the part of God is unappreciated by his people (32:15 – 18). How could such an emphatic, energetic exercise of divine love not be reciprocated? Certainly one would expect that God's "energic Nun love" for his people would result in their "energic Nun love" for him! God's emphatic, energetic care and provision for his people would be most fully realized in Christ's incarnation, death, and resurrection on our behalf. And yet the New Testament makes it clear that even this exercise of God's energetic, emphatic love for his people occurred while we were not only failing to reciprocate his love but were actively sinning against him (Rom 5:8). If energic Nuns do, in fact, indicate heightened force or energy for the verbal action, then perhaps it is time for God's people to put an energic Nun into their love for God.

FEMININE

What It Looks Like

The feminine ending attaches to **noun**s and **adjective**s (including **participle**s, which are *verbal* adjectives). There are **singular** and **plural** feminine endings. The singular feminine endings include:

ה ָ as in מַלְכָּה (queen).

ת ֶ as in מֹלֶכֶת (reigning)

ת ַ as in דַּעַת (knowledge)

ות as in מַלְכוּת (kingship, realm)

The feminine plural ending is:

ות as in בָּנוֹת (daughters)

What It Does

The feminine ending marks the noun or adjective as grammatically feminine. Adjectives always give a true indication of their grammatical gender. So the presence of a feminine ending on an adjective will always indicate a grammatically feminine form. Some Hebrew nouns, however, are grammatically feminine even though they don't have a feminine ending. Also, some **masculine** nouns may take the feminine plural ending, even though they remain grammatically masculine. Although there are numerous and significant exceptions, for most nouns the presence of the feminine ending will be a reliable indicator of a grammatically feminine form.

An Exegetical Insight

Recognizing feminine endings can help resolve potential ambiguities in English translations. For example, an English translation of the Hebrew in the first half of Obadiah 17 is: "But on Mount Zion will be deliverance; it will be holy." This leaves the reader with an ambiguity regarding the referent of "holy." Is the verse saying that *Mount Zion* will be something that is holy, or that the *deliverance* will be something that is holy? These two possibilities lead to significantly different exegetical conclusions. But knowing the Hebrew feminine ending resolves the ambiguity.

The Hebrew word translated as "deliverance" is פְּלֵיטָה (with the feminine ending ָה). The Hebrew word translated as "holy" is קֹדֶשׁ (no feminine ending). We may accurately conclude, therefore, that "deliverance" is feminine gender and "holy" is not. Consequently, "holy" cannot be referring to "deliverance," because adjectives must always agree in gender with what they are modifying. Therefore, "holy" must instead be referring to "Mount Zion," which also lacks a feminine ending. Many English translations helpfully attempt to clarify this referent in their translations of this verse. The NET Bible, for example, translates "... and it will be a holy *place* once again" (italics added). The "deliverance," as welcome and miraculous as it will be, is not what is being described as "holy." Rather it is *Mount Zion* that will be holy, because that is where God will reside once more. And where God is, there is life and holiness. Once again, access to the Hebrew text has resulted in disambiguation.

HIPHIL

What It Looks Like

The Hiphil **verb stem** has some characteristic features in each of its **conjugation**s that enable one to differentiate it from other Hebrew verb stems.

- For most verbs in the **Perfect** conjugation:

  The three-**consonant root** will be preceded by the consonant הִ followed by a Hireq or Segol (that is, הִ or הֶ).

- For most verbs in the **Imperfect**, **Cohortative**, and **Jussive** conjugations:

  The three-consonant root will be preceded by the normal preformative consonants of the Imperfect, Jussive, or Cohortative followed by a Patakh (that is, יַ, תַּ, אַ, or נַ). There will also usually be a Hireq Yod or Tsere between the second and third root consonants. For example, we can recognize that the verb יַשְׁמִיר is a Hiphil Imperfect (third **person**, **masculine**, **singular**, or 3ms) because it has a normal preformative consonant for the Imperfect, followed by a Patakh (יַ). Also, there is a Hireq Yod between the second and third root consonants (that is, between the מ and the ר).

- For the **Imperative** conjugation:

  The preformative consonant of the second person Imperfect conjugation is replaced by a הַ. For example, the Hiphil Imperative 2mp of the root שׁמר is הַשְׁמִירוּ (the 2mp Hiphil Imperfect is תַּשְׁמִירוּ).

- The **Infinitive Construct** and **Infinitive Absolute** look almost identical to the masculine singular Hiphil Imperative.

- For the **Participle** form of most verbs:

  The three-consonant root is preceded by מַ. Also, there will usually be a Hireq Yod between the second and third root consonants.

What It Does

The Hiphil verb stem suggests two main nuances:

- *Causing* (someone or something) to carry out the action of the verbal idea.

  For example, the verbal idea communicated by the three-consonant root שׁמע is "to hear." So the Hiphil Perfect 3ms form הִשְׁמִיעַ means "he caused (someone) to hear."

- *Declaring* (someone or something) *to be* the verbal idea.

  For example, the verbal idea communicated by the three-consonant root רשׁע is "to be guilty." So the Hiphil Perfect 3ms form הִרְשִׁיעַ means "he declared (someone) to be guilty."

An Exegetical Insight

The main verbal idea associated with the three-consonant root קרב is "to get closer, come near." So, in the Hiphil stem, the verb means *to cause* to get closer, *to cause* to come near. The Hiphil form of this verb is therefore very appropriate for contexts involving sacrifice, where worshipers bring their sacrifice near (or *cause* it to come closer) to God. In fact, sometimes this Hiphil verb is even translated "sacrifice" in these contexts. For example, in Ezra 8:35 we're told that the returned exiles "sacrificed" (הִקְרִיבוּ) burnt offerings to the God of Israel. Knowing this Hiphil form and its meaning helps us to understand that a sacrifice is something that is intended to be brought into the very presence of God. It is not a mechanical procedure, but rather one that is very personal. The sacrifice is "brought near" to God with the intention that the worshiper will thereby be "brought near" to God as well. This understanding enriches our appreciation of New Testament passages such as Ephesians 2:13, which informs us that "in Christ Jesus you who were once far away have been *brought near* by the blood of Christ" (italics added). Jesus brought himself near to the Father as a sacrifice for our sin so that we, too, could be brought near to him. Now, as "living sacrifices" (Romans 12:1), we seek to draw nearer to God in our daily lives. One could even say that, with respect to God, the Hiphil verb form of the root קרב is a shorthand description of the entire Christian life!

HISHTAPHEL

What It Looks Like

The Hishtaphel **verb stem** only occurs for one three-**consonant root**: חוה. The most distinctive identifying feature for this verb stem is a שת inserted between the three-consonant root and any preformative consonant. Examples of what this looks like for the forms of this verb that occur in the Hebrew Bible are:

- For the **Perfect conjugation** (3ms): הִשְׁתַּחֲוָה

    Notice the שת between the root חוה and the preformative ה.

- For the **Imperfect** conjugation (3ms): יִשְׁתַּחֲוֶה

    Notice the שת between the root חוה and the preformative י.

- For the **Jussive** conjugation (3mp): יִשְׁתַּחוּ

    Notice the שת between the root חוה and the preformative י.

- For the **Imperative** conjugation (2mp): הִשְׁתַּחֲווּ

    Notice the שת between the root חוה and the preformative ה.

- For the **Infinitive Construct** conjugation: הִשְׁתַּחֲוֹת

    Notice the שת between the root חוה and the preformative ה.

- For the **Participle** conjugation (ms): מִשְׁתַּחֲוֶה

    Notice the שת between the root חוה and the preformative מ.

What It Does

The Hishtaphel verb stem denotes an action that one causes oneself to do. For example, if the sentence "I made myself swallow the disgusting food" were written in Hebrew, the verb "swallow" would be in the Hishtaphel verb stem because it is something I caused myself to do. The only root in which the Hishtaphel verb stem is found (חוה) has the general meaning "to bow down." So, in the Hishtaphel verb stem, it means "to cause oneself to bow down, to prostrate oneself."

An Exegetical Insight

In Psalm 99, the palmist is celebrating the fact that the Lord is the great and holy king over "all the nations" (99:2). Consequently, the psalmist urges all people to give to God the praise that is his due. In verse 5, the psalmist directs everyone to "exalt the LORD our God and worship at his footstool." Our understanding of this directive is deepened when we see that the verb translated as "worship" is the Hishtaphel **masculine plural** imperative of the root חוה.

The use of this verb stem communicates that the psalmist is inviting all people to consciously, willingly *submit themselves* to the authority of the Lord. The action envisioned is not something that is to be imposed upon people by an external force. It is rather something that the psalmist is encouraging everyone to *cause themselves* to do. It is only when people willingly bring themselves to place their lives at the feet of the Lord in humble submission to his will can they say that they are truly worshiping. Of course, the only human being who did this perfectly was Jesus Christ, whose "food" it was to do the will of the Father (John 4:34). When we yield to the transforming work of the spirit of Jesus Christ at work within us, we too will increasingly be able to submit ourselves to God's gracious, wise, and powerful will. The apostle Paul tells us that offering ourselves to God in this way is, indeed, our "true and proper worship" (Rom 12:1). True worship comes from the inside, from an intentional bending of one's will to the authority of God. One could even say that true worship is Hishtaphel worship.

HITPAEL

(Hitpalel, Hitpalpel, Hitpoel, Hitpolel)

What It Looks Like

There are several characteristic features of the Hitpael **verb stem** that enable one to differentiate it from other Hebrew verb stems:

- A **Dagesh** in the second **consonant** of the three-consonant **root** of the verb.

- A Patakh under the first consonant of the three-consonant root.

- At least a תְ before the three-consonant root (for further preformative elements, see below).

- In the **Perfect**, **Imperative**, **Infinitive Absolute**, or **Infinitive Construct** conjugations, the three-consonant root will be preceded by הִתְ.

- In the **Participle** conjugation, the three-consonant root will be preceded by מִתְ.

Many variations of this basic pattern are possible (see subheading above) when the three-consonant root has a long middle **vowel**, contains a **guttural** consonant, or has the same consonant for its second and third letters. These occasional variations in form, however, do not suggest departures from the basic nuances of the Hitpael, described below.

What It Does

The Hitpael verb stem suggests three main nuances:

- A reflexive sense; that is, the action of the verb is done to the subject of the verb by the subject of the verb. For example, the verbal idea communicated by the three-consonant root קדשׁ is "to be holy, set apart." So the Hitpael Perfect 3ms form הִתְקַדֵּשׁ means "he made himself holy/set apart"; or, in smoother English, "he sanctified or consecrated *himself*."

- A reciprocal sense; that is, the action of the verb is done by multiple subjects to or with each other. For example, the verbal idea communicated by the three-consonant root קָשַׁר is "to conspire." So the Hitpael Perfect 3cp form, הִתְקַשְּׁרוּ means "they conspired *with each other/together*."
- An iterative sense; that is, the action of the verb is done repeatedly. For example, the verbal idea communicated by the three-consonant root הָלַךְ is "to walk." So the Hitpael Perfect 3ms form הִתְהַלֵּךְ means "he walked *around/back and forth*."

An Exegetical Insight

In Job 1:7 and 2:2, when the Lord asks Satan where he has come from, Satan replies, "From roaming throughout the earth, going back and forth on it." The phrase "going back and forth" translates a Hitpael Infinitive Construct: הִתְהַלֵּךְ. This is the iterative sense of the Hitpael. It communicates the scary truth that Satan doesn't just occasionally venture forth from his dark domain to see what damage he can do on the earth. No, his activity is continuous and relentless. So the apostle Peter describes the devil as a roaring lion prowling around "looking for someone to devour" (1 Pet 5:8).

Against this iterative threat, news of a divine, protective Hitpael is most welcome. In Leviticus 26:12, God informs his people that only in relationship with him is where their safety from Satan's slithery schemes can be found. That's because God's gracious presence is also continuous and relentless. In this verse, God says: "I will walk among you [וְהִתְהַלַּכְתִּי] and be your God, and you will be my people." The use of a Hitpael form of the same three-consonant root (הָלַךְ) assures us that God's care and protection are as powerfully enduring as he is and more than a match for Satan's malevolent iterative activity.

HOPHAL

What It Looks Like

The Hophal **verb stem** occurs most frequently in the **Perfect**, **Imperfect**, and **Participle conjugation**s. It has several characteristic features in these conjugations that enable one to differentiate it from other Hebrew verb stems.

- For the Perfect conjugation, the three-**consonant root** will be preceded by the consonant ה followed by a Qibbuts or a Qamets Khatuf (that is, הֻ or הָ). For example, we can recognize that the verb הָשְׁלַךְ is a Hophal Perfect (third **person**, **masculine**, **singular**, or 3ms) because there is a הָ in front of the three-consonant root שׁלך.

- For the Imperfect conjugation, the three-consonant root will be preceded by the normal preformative consonants of the Imperfect, followed by a Qibbuts or a Qamets Khatuf (that is, יֻ or יָ, תֻ or תָ, אֻ or אָ, and נֻ or נָ). For example, we can recognize that the verb תָּקְטַר is a Hophal Imperfect (third person, **feminine**, singular, or 3fs) because it has a normal preformative consonant for the Imperfect followed by a Qamets Khatuf (תָּ).

- For the Participle, the three-consonant root is preceded by מֻ or מָ. For example, we can recognize that the form מָשְׁזָר is a Hophal Participle (masculine, singular) because there is a מָ in front of the three-consonant root שׁזר.

What It Does

The Hophal verb stem is the passive of the **Hiphil** verb stem. The Hiphil suggests either (1) to *cause* (someone or something) to carry out the action of the verbal idea, or (2) *to declare* (someone or something) to be the verbal idea. So, the Hophal would signify the passive of these two nuances:

- to *be caused* to carry out the action of the verbal idea, or
- to *be declared* to be the verbal idea.

An Exegetical Insight

The verbal idea surrounding the three-consonant root פקד is difficult to state concisely in English. It means something like "take special notice of, give careful attention to." When someone gives special attention to an individual or group it can be to fulfill a promise (God to Sarah in Gen 21:1), muster the troops (David in 2 Sam 18:1), or appoint someone to a special position (the call of Jeremiah in Jer 1:10). However, the special attention can also be for a more unpleasant purpose. For example, in the book of Jeremiah God informs his people that it is time that their sins are given the full attention they deserve. So in this book the root פקד is frequently translated as "punish" (for example, Jer 5:9, 29; 9:9 [Hebrew 9:8], 25 [Hebrew 9:24]; 14:10; etc.). But translating the verb in this way may obscure its deeper meaning: careful, judicious appraisal leading to action.

In Jeremiah 6:6 we encounter the only Hophal form of פקד in the book (הָפְקַד). In this verse the Lord says, "This city must be *punished*" (italics added). An amplified translation would be, "The sinful behavior of this city has merited my special attention." Notice the nuance of the Hophal. God's special attention *has been caused* by the sin of the people. But whose behavior has *not* caused this kind of terrifying divine special attention? Thankfully, there is one—Jesus Christ. And because of his faithful obedience, God through Jeremiah can later promise his people that instead of *being caused* to give their sins special attention, he will remember their sins no more (Jer 31:34). Now instead of God *being caused* to give our sin special attention, we have *been caused* to give God's grace special attention!

——— IMPERATIVE ———

What It Looks Like

The form of the Imperative **verb** in any of Hebrew's seven verb **stems** is based on the form of the **Imperfect conjugation**. Because the Imperative only occurs in second-**person** forms (that is, "you" **masculine** or **feminine**, **singular** or **plural**), its form will be the same as (or very similar to) the corresponding second-person Imperfect form without its preformative elements. For example:

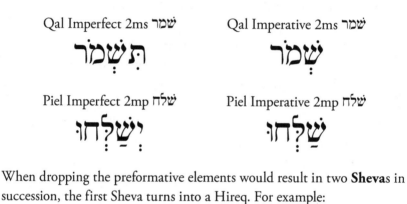

When dropping the preformative elements would result in two **Sheva**s in succession, the first Sheva turns into a Hireq. For example:

What It Does

The Imperative is a volitional conjugation. That means it represents the will (or volition) of the speaker. By means of its distinctive forms, the Imperative conjugation usually indicates that the will of the speaker is being expressed by means of a command. For example, when the root שׁמר, meaning "to guard," occurs in the Imperative conjugation, we translate it as a command: "Guard!"

An Exegetical Insight

Many people, Christians and non-Christians, use the term "Hallelujah!" to mean something like "What a relief!" or "Fantastic!" What they probably don't realize, however, is that they are using a Hebrew Imperative. The expression, "Hallelujah," is made up of two Hebrew words: הַלְלוּ (hallelu) and יָהּ (yah). The first of these words, hallelu, is a Piel Imperative (mp) from the root הלל, meaning "to praise." The second word in the expression, yah, is a short form of the divine covenantal name *Yahweh*. When people say "Hallelujah," then, they are actually giving a command to those around them to "Praise the LORD!" So, contrary to popular understanding, "Hallelujah" is not properly an expression of relief or excitement; it is an expression of praise directed toward the One who has provided the circumstances that produced the relief or excitement. It is an acknowledgement of God's providential care, coming even from the mouths of those who refuse to submit to his lordship. How wonderful!

Psalm 148 begins and ends with "Praise the LORD" (הַלְלוּ יָהּ) to indicate that everyone and everything contained within the psalm falls under the force of this command. Among those listed are "young men and women, old men and children" (148:12). In other words, *everyone* on earth is commanded to give God the praise that is his due. Hallelujah!

IMPERFECT

(Prefix Conjugation, Preformative Conjugation, YQTL Conjugation)

What It Looks Like

An Imperfect **verb** is recognized by means of the **consonants** (called preformatives) that attach to the *front* of the three-consonant **root**. That's why this **conjugation** is also called the "*pre*formative" conjugation. Some forms also have consonants and **vowels** that attach to the end of the three-consonant root. Only the features of the Imperfect conjugation that are shared by all of Hebrew's seven verb stems are shown below, attached to boxes that represent the consonants of any three-consonant root:

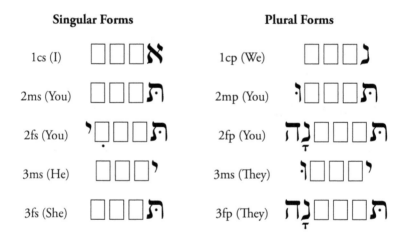

	Singular Forms		Plural Forms
1cs (I)	□□□א	1cp (We)	□□□נ
2ms (You)	□□□ת	2mp (You)	ו□□□ת
2fs (You)	י□□□ת	2fp (You)	הנָ□□□ת
3ms (He)	□□□י	3ms (They)	ו□□□י
3fs (She)	□□□ת	3fp (They)	הנָ□□□ת

What It Does

The Imperfect conjugation indicates that the action of the verb is not complete. We usually indicate this incomplete action in English by the present or future tenses. The incomplete action signaled by the Imperfect conjugation may also be habitual or customary action. For example, the verbal phrase "used to sell" in the sentence "I used to sell magazines door-to-door" would be indicated in Hebrew by the Imperfect conjugation because the action, even though it took place in the past, was ongoing. It is also important to note that a verb in the Imperfect conjugation may be translated with a modal value, that is, preceded by "would," "could," "should," "may," "might," and so forth. Context is the ultimate determining factor for which one of these translational options applies.

An Exegetical Insight

In Exodus 3:14 Moses asks God to tell him what to say to the people when they ask who sent Moses to them. God tells Moses, "This is what you are to say to the Israelites: '[אֶהְיֶה] has sent me to you.'" The three-consonant root היה (meaning "to be") has an א in front of it, indicating that it is a 1cs Imperfect verb, so the subject of the verb is "I." But how should we translate the verbal idea? "I *will be*"? "I *am*"? "I *have been*"? The answer is yes, yes, and yes. Because the basic sense of the verb is "to exist," and God has always existed and always will exist, the Imperfect verb includes all of these senses. Indeed, elsewhere God describes himself as "the Alpha and Omega ... who is, and who was, and who is to come" (Revelation 1:8).

In English, however, our verbal system operates on the basis of time, unlike the Hebrew verbal system, which operates on the basis of whether or not the action is regarded as completed. So how can we translate this Hebrew verb that indicates continuing existence unrestricted by time into the English language, where action is expressed in terms of the time in which it occurs? Well, we do the best we can. Most English translations opt for the present tense and render the designation God gives himself as "I AM." Recognizing the significance of the Hebrew Imperfect conjugation, however, gives the reader the advantage of seeing that God is describing himself not just as being present *then*, but rather as being continually present. The omnipresence of God is an essential foundation of a believer's confidence. And it provides a greater depth of understanding for the "I am" in the words of the Son of God at the end of Matthew's gospel (28:20): "And surely I am with you always, to the very end of the age."

INFINITIVE ABSOLUTE

What It Looks Like

The Infinitive Absolute **conjugation** usually has only one form for each of the seven **verb stem**s in Hebrew. The exceptions are the **Niphal** and **Piel** verb stem, which have two possibilities. The form for each verb stem is shown below, attached to boxes that represent the **consonants** of any three-consonant **root**:

Verb Stem	Infinitive Absolute
Qal	☐ ו ☐ ☐
Niphal	☐ ו ☐ נְ or ☐ ו ☐ ☐ הָ
Hiphil	☐ ☐ ☐ ה
Hophal	none
Piel	☐ ו ☐ ☐ or ☐ ☐ ☐
Pual	none
Hitpael	☐ ☐ ☐ הִתְ

What It Does

Usually, the Infinitive Absolute comes immediately before or after the main verb in the sentence and modifies that verb in some way. If it comes *after* the main verb, then it is describing adverbially the action of the main verb. In the English sentence, "He drove while texting," the word "texting" would be an Infinitive Absolute in Hebrew. If the Infinitive Absolute comes *before* the main verb, then it is emphasizing the action of the main verb. In the English sentence, "I really like ice cream," the word "really" would be an Infinitive Absolute in Hebrew. Less frequently, the Infinitive Absolute stands in place of the main verb in the sentence.

An Exegetical Insight

The English translation of Psalm 49:7–8 [Hebrew 49:8–9] reads: "No one can redeem the life of another or give to God a ransom for them—the ransom for a life is costly, no payment is ever enough." If you examine the Hebrew for these verses, you'll see that the verb "redeem" (יִפְדֶּה—a **Qal Imperfect** 3ms from the root פדה) is preceded by an Infinitive Absolute of the same root: פָּדֹה. The occurrence of the Infinitive Absolute *before* the main verb of the same root signals the fact that the main verb is being emphasized. One might capture this emphasis in more casual English, then, by translating the first part of verse 7 as, "*It's just not possible* for a person to redeem the life of someone else." This emphasis helps us to understand our desperate situation even more deeply. If there is absolutely nothing we human beings can do to bring about our redemption, then what hope do we have? Thankfully, God in his relentless grace has solved the problem for us. God incredibly and mysteriously became a sinless human being in Jesus Christ to do what we could not. Because he is perfect, he alone *is* able to do what no other human being can possibly do: "redeem the life of another [and] give to God a ransom for them." We will never fully appreciate the unbreakable new-covenant relationship we can have with God by faith in Jesus Christ until we come to grips with the full implications of the Infinitive Absolute in this verse.

INFINITIVE CONSTRUCT

What It Looks Like

The Infinitive Construct **conjugation** has only one main form for each of the seven **verb stem**s in Hebrew. And the form is usually identical to the second-person, masculine singular **Imperative** form in each of those conjugations. The form of the Infinitive Construct is shown below for each verb stem in which it occurs with significant frequency. The boxes represent the **consonant**s of any three-consonant **root**:

Verb Stem	Imperative (for illustration purposes)	Infinitive Construct
Qal	☐☐☐	☐☐☐
Niphal	הִ☐☐☐	הִ☐☐☐
Hiphil	הַ☐☐יַ☐	הַ☐☐☐
Piel	☐☐☐	☐☐☐
Hitpael	הִתְ☐☐☐	הִתְ☐☐☐

What It Does

The Infinitive Construct signifies action that is functioning as a **noun** rather than a verb. For example, if I say "*Smoking* in class is prohibited," the word "smoking" is functioning as a noun (as the subject of the sentence). In fact, I could use a noun in its place: "*Matches* in class are prohibited."

So, an Infinitive Construct is often translated as a noun that ends with -ing. It can also be translated as an English infinitive (preceded by "to"). For example, in the sentence above, I could communicate the same idea as "*Smoking* in class is prohibited" by using an English infinitive: "*To smoke* in class is prohibited." Infinitive Constructs differ from regular nouns in that they can also have a direct object. For example, I could say "Smoking (or, To smoke) *cigars* in class is prohibited."

An Exegetical Insight

In 1 Samuel 15:22, when Samuel rebukes Saul for his disobedience to God's command, he uses Infinitive Constructs to do so: "To obey [שְׁמֹעַ] is better than sacrifice, and to heed [הַקְשִׁיב] is better than the fat of rams." Note the nouns that are being compared: "to obey/obeying" is compared with "sacrifice," and "to heed/heeding" is compared with "the fat of rams." In both cases, the first noun (the Infinitive Construct) is judged to be better. The Infinitive Constructs are denoting action in a noun form. So, by using Infinitive Constructs, Samuel is communicating to Saul that the behavior/action that characterizes his relationship with the Lord is of primary importance. The general behavior from which the specific sacrifices proceed has far greater importance to God than the sacrifices themselves. Saul's illegitimate sacrifices are concrete expressions of a pattern of behavior that is far from where it should be. The Infinitive Constructs inform us that God desires obeying and attentively responding to his word to be ongoing, accurate descriptors of his people. How that obedience and attentive response are manifested in particular situations may change, but their presence should not. Thankfully, Jesus' perfect obedience is attributed to us through our faith in him so that the Infinitive Constructs of 1 Samuel 15:22 are always counted as true for us.

INTERJECTION

(Exclamation)

What It Looks Like

A Hebrew interjection has no distinguishing features that enable us to differentiate it from other kinds of words. It has no markers for **person**, gender, or number. One must either learn interjections as vocabulary words or depend on Bible software or other Hebrew language resources for their identification.

What It Does

A Hebrew interjection performs the same functions as an English interjection. An interjection is an audible expression of an emotion or feeling (usually strong) that is often an involuntary, audible reaction to something perceived or felt. English examples include "Ah!," Aha!," "Ew!," "Ugh!," and "D'oh!"

An Exegetical Insight

Because interjections are often expressive of an underlying emotion, they can give us insight into the biblical author's mental state that might be otherwise unavailable to us. And knowing the sounds of the Hebrew **consonant**s and **vowel**s enables us to virtually hear the biblical author expressing his emotional reaction as if we were there.

In Amos 5:16, for example, in a context that describes the anguish expressed in the aftermath of the Lord's judgment, we find the interjection הוֹ (*ho*) repeated twice. Unfortunately, in English "Ho! Ho!" sounds like something Santa would say—hardly indicating an expression of grief. Therefore, most modern English translations attempt to communicate the grief expressed by this interjection with a more explanatory rendering. So, for example, the NIV translates this part of the verse as "There will be ... *cries of anguish*" (italics added). The NET translates it as "They *will mourn the dead*" (italics added). The HCSB has "They *will cry out in anguish*" (italics added). The NLT has "There will be ... *mourning*" (italics added).

These examples illustrate a problem translations frequently face. Should the interjection be rendered in equivalent English letters, even if it will perhaps communicate something different than it does in Hebrew? Or should the English translation attempt to communicate the force or meaning of the Hebrew interjection (as illustrated by the examples above)? Or should the Hebrew interjection be translated instead by an English interjection that has a similar meaning? The ESV chooses the latter option and renders these two Hebrew interjections as "Alas! Alas!"

When readers are able to recognize Hebrew interjections, all the translational options remain available to them. And being able to pronounce the Hebrew interjections enables one to hear the raw emotion of the biblical author as he would have expressed it himself, unfiltered through an English translation.

─── INTERROGATIVE ───

What It Looks Like

There are three kinds of interrogative words in Hebrew. As is the case in English, all of these will usually be the first element in their clause:

1) Interrogative **pronoun**s: מִי "who?" and מַה "what?"
2) Interrogative **adverb**s:

- לָמָּה "why?" (a combination of the inseparable **preposition** לְ and מַה)
- אֵי (also אַיֵּה, אָן and אַיִן) "where?"
- אֵיךְ (also אֵיכָה) "how?"
- מָתַי "when?"

3) An interrogative **particle** הֲ (before a **guttural consonant**: הַ or הֶ). Unlike English, where the question mark indicates a question by attaching directly to the end of the last word in a sentence, the Hebrew "question mark" (הֲ) attaches directly to the front of the first word in a sentence. For example, the Hebrew sentence הַמֶּלֶךְ דָּוִד ("David is the king") can be made into a question by adding the interrogative particle הֲ at the beginning: הֲדָוִד הַמֶּלֶךְ ("Is David the king?").

What It Does

The presence of a Hebrew interrogative word or particle simply indicates that a question is being asked.

An Exegetical Insight

The names of people and places in Hebrew are often sentences whose meaning is not obvious in English translations. Sometimes these name-sentences include an interrogative. For example, the name of the prophet Micah (מִיכָה) is a shorter form of the name Michael, which means "Who is like God?"—a rhetorical question with the obvious answer, "No one!" Micah's full name, Michael (מִיכָאֵל), has three parts: (1) the interrogative pronoun מִי ("who"), (2) the inseparable preposition כְּ ("like"), and (3) the **noun** אֵל, meaning "God." Often in Hebrew names containing an element referring to God, that part will be removed in shortened forms of the name. So, in this case, when the divine element (אֵל) of Micah's name is removed, we end up with Micah (מִיכָה), a shortened form of Michael (מִיכָאֵל).

Knowing the meaning of his name gives us insight into Micah's rhetorical question in Micah 7:18. In this passage, Micah is rejoicing over the fact of God's mercy and forgiveness. Our understanding of interrogatives enables us to hear Micah's question on a deeper level. In the middle of his praise, Micah is no doubt exegeting the meaning of his own name when he asks: "Who is a God like you" (מִי־אֵל כָּמוֹךָ)—a rhetorical question with the obvious answer, "No one!" The very presence of this prophet of God is a reminder to all who know his name that their covenant God is beyond compare.

JUSSIVE

What It Looks Like

The form of the Jussive **verb** in any of Hebrew's seven verb **stems** is often identical to the third-**person** form of the **Imperfect conjugation**. When possible, however, the Jussive form will be a modified form of the third-person Imperfect form. This modification will occur whenever the three-**consonant root** ends with a ה, has a long middle **vowel**, or is in the **Hiphil** verb stem. Note the differences below between the third-person Imperfect forms and the Jussive forms in these cases where such modification occurs:

Qal Imperfect 3ms עשה

יַעֲשֶׂה

Qal Jussive 3ms עשה

יַעַשׂ

Notice how the final ה of the root has dropped off (= apocopation) in the Jussive

Qal Imperfect 3ms שוב

יָשׁוּב

Qal Jussive 3ms שוב

יָשֹׁב

Notice how the Shureq has changed to a Holem in the Jussive

Hiphil Imperfect 3ms שמד

יַשְׁמִיד

Hiphil Jussive 3ms שמד

יַשְׁמֵד

Notice how the Hireq Yod has changed to a Tsere in the Jussive

What It Does

The Jussive is a volitional conjugation. That means it represents the will (or volition) of the speaker. Because it only occurs in third-person forms, it indicates the speaker wishes to impose their will onto a third-person entity (that is, onto "him," "her," "it," or "them"). For example, the translation of the Jussive forms in the examples above would be (1) "Let him (or it) make/do"; (2) "Let him (or it) return"; and (3) "Let him (or it) destroy."

An Exegetical Insight

The idea communicated by the Jussive can be a little difficult for English speakers to get their heads around. We're used to giving commands in the second person: "Do this!" "Do that!" But the idea of giving commands in the third person might be a little unfamiliar. Nevertheless, we have ways we regularly communicate this idea in everyday language: "*Let him* cook supper himself if he doesn't like my cooking!" "If she doesn't like my work, then *let her* do it herself!" In these examples, the speaker is expressing his will to have a third person do something without speaking directly to that person. Don't allow the use of the word "let" (that often begins translations of the jussive) fool you. "Let" in these cases does not signify granting permission; it signifies an assertion of the will.

Consider Psalm 150:6, the last verse in the book of Psalms. By the time we get to the end of verse 5 we've encountered the **Piel Imperative** 2mp ("Praise!") no less than eleven times! One might say that these verses are "command rich"! Then we get to the last verse, the first part of which begins with the words, "Let everything that has breath praise the Lord." This is not a pious wish, as if the psalmist meant "We mustn't hinder anyone from praising the Lord." Rather, this is a Jussive form, indicating that the palmist is continuing to command. Instead of continuing to use the second-person Imperative forms that have specified where, why, and how to praise God, the psalmist shifts to the third-person Jussive form in this last verse in order to specify "who" should praise God: "everything that has breath." The Jussive form clears away any ambiguity. None of us is exempt from the responsibility to give God the praise that he deserves. So, *let him* be praised!

KETIB-QERE

What It Looks Like

A Ketib-Qere can be recognized when a word appears to depart from the normal Hebrew **consonant** and **vowel** pattern. This signals a textual issue or problem. For example, a common Ketib-Qere is the form הוא. The fact that the consonant Waw is never preceded by a Hireq in Hebrew should alert the reader to the fact that something unusual is happening here. As a further aid in recognizing these phenomena, the problematic word in the Hebrew text of the *Biblia Hebraica Stuttgartensia* (BHS; the standard Hebrew text of the Old Testament) will have a small circle above it. In the margin at that point in the text you will find the consonants of the word as it was heard in the oral tradition.

What It Does

The Masoretes were Jewish scholars who later added vowels (or, "vowel points") to the Hebrew text that was originally comprised exclusively of consonants. This vowel pointing reflected the oral tradition as it existed when the Masoretes worked (ca. AD 6th–10th centuries). At times, the oral tradition the Masoretes were seeking to preserve by means of vowel points conflicted with the consonantal text that was in front of them. This is where the Ketib-Qere comes in. The name is simply the transliteration of two Aramaic words. The first, Ketib, means "written." It reflects the consonantal text the Masoretes inherited. The second word, Qere, means "read." It reflects the oral tradition the Masoretes were seeking to preserve. Because of their reverence for the consonantal text, the Masoretes would never alter it. Instead, they wrote the vowels of the word they heard in the oral tradition around the consonantal text that was in front of them. This can result in some strange forms.

For example, in the Hebrew text of Genesis 24:33, the word וַיִּישֶׂם is a Ketib-Qere. We can recognize that it is such by the fact that a Qibbuts is never followed by a Yod in Hebrew, and also because there is a small circle above the word (noted in BHS). If we look in the margin of BHS, we find the consonants וְיֹשֶׁם, indicating that the Masoretes were *hearing* וַיּוּשָׁם, despite what the consonantal tradition is indicating.

An Exegetical Insight

A common Ketib-Qere in biblical Hebrew is the word יְהֹוָה (or its more common abbreviated form, יְהוָה). Clearly, in the many cases where it occurs, the consonantal tradition is indicating that the divine covenantal name יהוה (probably pronounced "Yahweh") is intended. However, out of reverence, and to avoid unintentionally violating the third commandment, this proper **noun** was never pronounced. In its place the generic noun אֲדֹנָי ("lord") was spoken. To indicate this difference, the Masoretes took the vowels of the generic noun and placed them around the consonants of the proper noun. This results in the hybrid form יְהֹוָה. To attempt to pronounce this hybrid form is to follow neither the consonantal tradition nor the oral tradition. Yet, this is exactly what has happened in English! Older Bible translations and hymns frequently use the term *Yehovah* or *Jehovah*—a word that would have confused any devout Israelite! In Genesis 17:1, for example, it is the personal God, Yahweh (יהוה), who appears to Abraham and makes the precious covenant with him. And it is the personal God, Jesus, who has secured our covenantal relationship with God.

Most English Bibles use the form Lord to indicate when this proper noun—God's personal, covenantal name—occurs in the Hebrew text. When you encounter this term, don't let the unintended consequences of a Ketib-Qere obscure the deeper significance, obvious in the Hebrew. Remember that יהוה is the name of a *personal* God who is seeking a personal relationship with you.

——— MASCULINE ———

What It Looks Like

Unlike the **feminine singular**, the masculine singular has no ending attached to the lexical form. The masculine **plural** form of **noun**s and **adjective**s (including **participle**s, which are verbal adjectives) is recognized by the ending ‎ים . Consider the examples below:

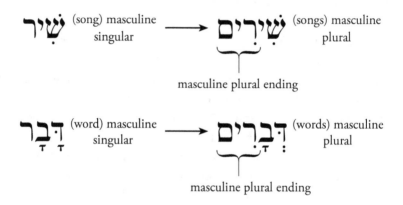

In the second example, the initial Qamets changed to a **Sheva** when the masculine plural ending was added. For an explanation for why this is so, see the Appendix entitled The Effect of the Accent on Vowels at the end of this resource.

What It Does

The lack of additional ending (for masculine singular nouns) or the presence of a masculine plural ending marks the noun or adjective as grammatically masculine. Adjectives always give a true indication of their grammatical gender. Some Hebrew nouns, however, are grammatically masculine plural even though they may have a feminine plural ending. Also, some feminine nouns may take the masculine plural ending even though they remain grammatically feminine. Although there are numerous and significant exceptions, for most nouns the lack of any ending in the singular or the presence of the masculine plural ending will be a reliable indicator of a grammatically masculine form.

An Exegetical Insight

A feature of Hebrew grammatical gender attribution that may be misleading for English readers is that groups that are a mix of masculine and feminine people or animals are always referred to with masculine terms. For example, Proverbs 6:19 lists among the things that are detestable to the Lord: וּמְשַׁלֵּחַ מְדָנִים בֵּין אַחִים ("a person who stirs up conflict in the community"). Notice that the last word in this clause has the masculine plural ending (ים ָ). The singular form of the word is usually translated as "brother." But in this context, a group that includes both males and females is clearly in view. Otherwise, one would have to conclude that the Lord considers it detestable when one stirs up conflict among brothers, but he's not so concerned if the conflict is stirred up among sisters. Of course, such a translation misses the point entirely. Nevertheless, some contemporary English translations translate the word this way. However, those translations that are more concerned with communicating the correct meaning instead of reflecting a Hebrew grammatical practice that is foreign to English have translated אַחִים in this verse in a way that reflects the fact that the group referred to is composed of both males and females. For example, the NIV renders this word as "the community"; the NET renders it as "family members"; and the NLT renders it as "a family."

Being aware of the way Hebrew uses the masculine gender as a "group gender" can safeguard the reader against misinterpretations that incorrectly exclude half the population. We can assert with confidence and gratitude that God's concern for his covenant community extends to both males and females!

NEGATING PARTICLE

(Negative Particle, the General Negative, Negative Adverb)

What It Looks Like

The most common negating particles are לֹא, אַל, בַּל, and בִּלְתִּי. Each of these words occurs in specific contexts and has no markers for **person**, gender, or number. The most common negating particle in the Hebrew text, לֹא, which occurs several thousand times, is discussed below, but many of its characteristics are shared by other negating particles as well.

What It Does

The negating particle has three main functions:

- It negates the word it (usually immediately) precedes.

  לֹא יָדַע He did not know (Judg 16:20)

  הִיא לֹא אִשְׁתִּי She is not my wife (Hos 2:2 [Hebrew 2:4])

  לֹא־טוֹב It is not good (Gen 2:18)

- It can stand alone as a (usually emphatic) negative response to a question.

  וַיֹּאמֶר אֲלֵהֶם מְרַגְּלִים אַתֶּם וַיֹּאמְרוּ אֵלָיו לֹא אֲדֹנִי

  Then he said to them, "You are spies!" ... "No, my lord," they answered (Gen 42:9–10)

- It is used with an **apocopated** second-person **Imperfect verb** to form a negative command or prohibition with durative force.

  לֹא תִּגְנֹבוּ Do not steal (Lev 19:11)

  (The negating particle אַל is used in a similar way for a non-durative prohibition.)

An Exegetical Insight

A striking use of the negating particle is found in the prophecy of Hosea. Hosea had been given the unpleasant task of prophesying God's judgment against the northern kingdom of Israel during its last days. Hosea accomplishes his task through both his words and his life. As part of Hosea's prophetic communication, he is instructed to give names to his children that indicate God's coming judgment against the nation.

Two of these names include the negating particle: Lo-Ruhamah (לֹא רֻחָמָה, "not loved") and Lo-Ammi (לֹא עַמִּי, "not my people"). What a shock for the nation to realize that their God, who had historically referred to them as "my people," should now prophetically use these names! Consider, for example, the encounters between God's representatives, Moses and Aaron, and Pharaoh in the book of Exodus. No less than seven times Moses and Aaron relay God's command to Pharaoh, "Let my people go" (שַׁלַּח עַמִּי, Exod 5:1; 7:16; 8:1 [Hebrew 7:26], 20 [Hebrew 8:16]; 9:1, 13; 10:3). Now Hosea must inform them that the God who had claimed them as his own by addressing them as "my people" now precedes that term of endearment with the negating particle לֹא.

Yet, in the same book, God graciously promises that a day is coming when "I will show my love to the one I called 'Not my loved one.' I will say to those called 'Not my people [לֹא עַמִּי]' 'You are my people [עַמִּי]'" (Hos 2:23 [Hebrew 2:25]). The apostle Peter informs us that the day Hosea prophesied is realized for those who come to God through faith in Jesus Christ. In 1 Peter 2:10, he informs believers that "Once you were *not a people*, but now you are the people of God" (italics added). Through faith in Jesus Christ, the negating particle is itself negated!

NIPHAL

What It Looks Like

The Niphal **verb stem** has some characteristic features in each of its **conjugation**s that enable one to differentiate it from other Hebrew verb stems.

- For most verbs in the **Perfect** conjugation:

  The three-**consonant root** will be preceded by the consonant נ followed by a Hireq or Segol (that is, נִ or נֶ).

- For most verbs in the **Imperfect**, **Cohortative**, and **Jussive** conjugations:

  The three-consonant root will be preceded by the normal preformative consonants of the Imperfect, Jussive, or Cohortative. But the first consonant of the three-consonant root will have a dot inside of it (a **Dagesh**) and a Qamets underneath it. Note these distinctive features in the following Niphal Imperfect 3ms verb:

יִשָּׁמֵר

Qamets under first consonant of the three-consonant root   Dagesh inside first consonant of the three-consonant root

- For the **Imperative** conjugation:

  The preformative consonant of the second person Imperfect Conjugation is replaced by a הֵ. For example, the Niphal Imperative 2mp of the root שׁמר is הִשָּׁמְרוּ (the 2mp Niphal Imperfect is תִּשָּׁמְרוּ).

- The **Infinitive Construct** is identical to the masculine singular Niphal Imperative.

- The Niphal **Infinitive Absolute** has two possible forms: נִ◌◌וֹ◌ or הִ◌◌ָ◌וֹ◌

- For the **Participle**, the three-consonant root is preceded by נ.

What It Does

The Niphal verb stem suggests two main nuances:

- Simple action with a passive voice; that is, the subject of the verb receives the action of the verb. For example, the verbal idea communicated by the three-consonant root שׁמר is "to guard." So the Niphal Perfect 3ms form נִשְׁמַר can mean "he was guarded."

- Simple action with a reflexive voice; that is, the subject of the verb performs the action of the verb upon him/her/itself. For example, the verbal idea communicated by the three-consonant root שׁמר is "to guard." So the Niphal Perfect 3ms form נִשְׁמַר can mean "he guarded himself."

Obviously, the context is determinative for which of these meanings applies.

An Exegetical Insight

The Niphal verb stem communicates a passive or reflexive voice. At times, however, which one of these is in view is not entirely clear. It may even be the case that in a particular context *both* perspectives may be intended — something not easily communicated in an English translation. Consider, for example, Hosea 8:4. The context of this verse is one of judgment. Among the ways God lists that his people have broken his covenant is the fact that they have made idols for themselves. The last word of this verse, the Niphal Imperfect verb יִכָּרֵת, spells out the consequences of this sinful act. The meaning of the root כרת in this context is "to destroy." But should the Niphal verb in this verse be understood as passive or reflexive? Will the nation "be destroyed," or will the nation by its sinful practice effectively "destroy itself"? Perhaps the answer is not either/or, but both/and. Sin brings its own negative consequences. God has set before us life and death (Deut 30:19). What we choose for ourselves (reflexive voice) will affect the future that will be experienced (passive voice) by us. God encourages us to "choose life" so that what is experienced by us is the life he wants for us.

NOUN

What It Looks Like

Hebrew nouns are either grammatically **masculine** or **feminine**. There is no neuter. A noun is also **singular**, **plural**, or **dual**. The gender and number of a noun can be recognized by its ending (or lack of the same). These endings are shown below:

	SINGULAR	PLURAL	DUAL
MASCULINE	no ending	ִים	ַיִם
FEMININE	ָה	וֹת	ָתַיִם

For example, we can recognize that דְּבָרִים is a masculine, plural noun because it ends with ִים. One should note, however, that sometimes a grammatically feminine noun will take a masculine ending, and vice versa. For example, שָׁנִים looks like a masculine plural noun because it ends with ִים. In actuality, it is a feminine plural noun, meaning "years." There is no way to recognize the true grammatical gender of these nouns apart from the lexical assistance available in Bible software programs or other Hebrew language resources.

What It Does

A noun refers to a person, place, or thing. A noun is called a "proper" noun if it is a formal name, for example, David. Otherwise it is a "common" noun. In a sentence, a noun can function as the subject, the direct object, the indirect object, or the object of a **preposition**. Examples of these are provided below:

- Subject of a sentence: בָּנָה אִישׁ A *man* built.
- Direct object of a **verb**: בָּנָה אִישׁ הֵיכָל A man built a *palace*.

- Indirect object of a verb: בָּנָה אִישׁ הֵיכָל לְמֶלֶךְ A man built a palace for a *king*.
- Object of a preposition: בָּנָה אִישׁ הֵיכָל לְמֶלֶךְ בְּכוּשׁ A man built a palace for a king in *Cush*.

An Exegetical Insight

Because language is inexact, one noun may be used to refer to different things in the speaker's world. Consider, for example, the English word "rock." Among other things, it can refer to a stone; a kind of music, candy, or salt; or what a rocking chair does. Sometimes this inexact character of language is used by the biblical narrator to suggest, hint, or foreshadow.

For example, Genesis 37 – 50 recounts the story of Joseph. It can be argued that the person who changes the most in this narrative is Judah. He begins by leading his brothers in the deception of their father regarding the fate of Joseph, whom he and his brothers have sold into slavery in order to be rid of this irritating brother loved most by his father. At the end of the story, Judah offers himself as a slave instead of the brother loved most by his father. The change in Judah's character begins in chapter 38 at the instigation of his daughter-in-law Tamar, who seduces him at the entrance of Enaim (פֶּתַח עֵינַיִם, 38:14). Depending on the context, the noun פֶּתַח can mean "opening," "entrance," or "doorway." The proper noun עֵינַיִם (Enaim) is identical to the common noun meaning "eyes." Perhaps, therefore, the narrator is hinting at the change that begins in Judah's character as a result of the eye-opening events that occur in association with a place called פֶּתַח עֵינַיִם, "the entrance to Enaim" or "the opening of eyes." Even humble nouns can suggest a deeper (but not different) understanding of the biblical text.

NUMBER,
CARDINAL

What It Looks Like

Cardinal numbers are simply numbers such as "one," "two," "three," etc. There are no unique identifying features for these numbers. One must either learn them as vocabulary words or depend on Bible software or other Hebrew language resources for their identification. The cardinal numbers are always written out fully in biblical Hebrew. While the cardinal numbers have no distinct features, they do have recognizable patterns:

1–10

- Numbers 1 and 2 agree with the gender of the counted **noun**.
- Numbers 3–9 will have the opposite gender of the counted noun.
- The counted noun may come before or after (usually) the number.
- The number may be in the **construct** form when it comes before the counted noun.

11–19

- The numbers 1–9 come before the number 10.
- The counted noun may come before or after the number.
- The numbers 10, 1, and 2 will agree in gender with the counted noun; numbers 3–9 will have the opposite gender of the counted noun.

20–90

- 20 is the **plural** form of the number 10.
- The other "tens" (30, 40, etc.) resemble their corresponding units with **masculine** plural endings. For example, שָׁלֹשׁ is 3; שְׁלֹשִׁים is 30.
- The counted noun may be in the **singular** or plural form and come before or after the number.

21–99

- These consist of the unit then the "ten" or the "ten" then the unit.
- 1 and 2 will agree in gender with the counted noun; numbers 3–9 will have the opposite gender of the counted noun.

- The counted noun may be in the singular or plural form and come before or after the number.

100 (מֵאָה)
- It too may be counted (for example "three hundred": שְׁלֹשׁ מֵאוֹת).

1000 (אֶלֶף)
- It too may be counted (for example "three thousand": שְׁלֹשֶׁת אֲלָפִים).

10,000 (רְבָבָה [usually] or רִבּוֹא)

What It Does

As in English, a Hebrew cardinal number simply specifies the amount of something.

An Exegetical Insight

Cardinal numbers are sometimes provided in the narrative to enable the reader to make connections between passages that might not otherwise be made. Consider, for example, the connection the New Testament itself makes between Jonah's *three* days and *three* nights "in the belly of the fish" (Jonah 1:17 [Hebrew 2:1]) and the Son of Man's *three* days and *three* nights "in the heart of the earth" (Matt 12:40).

Another such connection is apparently being made by means of cardinal numbers in the account of Joseph in the book of Genesis. In 42:1, we learn that Joseph was in prison "two full years" *after* he had correctly interpreted the dreams of Pharaoh's officials. It was likely, then, that he was summoned into Pharaoh's presence sometime during his third year of imprisonment. In 42:17, after Joseph is surprised by the appearance of his brothers in Egypt, he directs that they be imprisoned "for three days." By the clever use of numbers, the narrator is inviting the reader to see a connection between Joseph's experience and what Joseph causes his brothers to experience. In other words, he is giving them a little taste of their own medicine. A very careful reader might have seen this connection anyway, but the cardinal numbers make it more obvious.

NUMBER, ORDINAL

What It Looks Like

There are no unique identifying features for these numbers. One must either learn them as vocabulary words or depend on Bible software or other Hebrew language resources for their identification. The ordinal numbers are always written out fully in biblical Hebrew. Though the ordinal numbers have no distinct features, they do have recognizable patterns:

First – Tenth

- "First" has a distinct form (רִאשׁוֹנָא / רִאשׁוֹן).
- "Second" through "tenth" closely resemble the **masculine** forms of their corresponding **cardinal** numbers with the ending יִ for masculine forms and יִת for **feminine** forms. For example, חָמֵשׁ (or חֲמִשָּׁה) is the cardinal number "five"; חֲמִישִׁי (or חֲמִישִׁית) is the ordinal number "fifth."

All Other Ordinals

- The cardinal number is used for the ordinal as well.
- Context is determinative for whether a cardinal or ordinal number is intended.

What It Does

As in English, an ordinal number describes the place of something in a series; that is, its "order." Hence the name "ordinal."

An Exegetical Insight

Because ordinal numbers describe the place of something in a series, they are particularly useful in describing calendrical events; that is, in describing specific days in their relation to other days on a timeline. Ordinal numbers are often used in the Bible, therefore, to communicate specific dates of significance.

This grammatical feature provides a critical exegetical perspective for understanding the book of Haggai, who uses ordinal numbers to date his prophetic speeches. This prophet was called by God to encourage the returned exiles to get re-energized about rebuilding the temple in Jerusalem. They had begun the project as soon as they returned from Babylonian exile (539 BC), and had completed its foundation about three years later (536 BC). Yet, after this auspicious beginning, the reader may be surprised to note that, using ordinal numbers, Haggai dates all of his prophetic speeches within a four-month period in *520* BC—from the "*second* year of King Darius, on the *first* day of the *sixth* month" (1:1, italics added) to the "*twenty-fourth* day of the *ninth* month" (2:18, italics added).

The precise dating of Haggai's prophecies to days and months within the year 520 BC (August 29–December 18) reveals that the rebuilding project had languished over the intervening sixteen years and was in desperate need of revitalization. That Haggai's words had good effect is evidenced by the book of Ezra, which records that "the temple was completed on the *third* day of the month of Adar, in the *sixth* year of the reign of King Darius" (Ezra 6:15); that is, on March 12, 516 BC—only four years after Haggai prophesied to the returned exiles. The use of ordinal numbers in the communication of specific dates in the Hebrew text thus enables the reader to follow the mental, physical, and even spiritual struggles that militate against putting God *first*.

PARAGOGIC HE
(He Paragogicum)

What It Looks Like

The paragogic He consists of a ה ָ attached to the end of a word in Hebrew where it is not expected. In fact, the word "paragogic" means "to extend." So, the paragogic He "extends" the usual form of the word. The paragogic He most frequently occurs at the end of **masculine, singular Imperatives**. Consider the difference in form shown below between the **Qal**, imperative, masculine, singular form of שְׁמֹר with and without the paragogic He attached to the end:

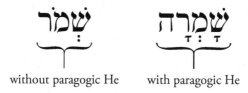

without paragogic He   with paragogic He

Note that the internal **vowel**s of the form with the paragogic He have been affected by the addition of this ending.

What It Does

The precise origin and meaning of the paragogic He is debated, so any statements regarding its function must remain tentative. The two most likely possibilities for its function are (1) that the paragogic He is a more polite form of address, when one of lower status requests action on the part of one of higher status, and (2) that the paragogic He is related to the ה ָ ending characteristic of the **Cohortative**, indicating, as does the Cohortative, a personal investment or interest on the speaker's part in the action that is being commanded.

An Exegetical Insight

The two possible functions of the paragogic He — a more polite address and a signal of the personal investment of the speaker — can both be observed in Psalm 86. In verse 2, the psalmist cries out to God: "Guard my life!" The verb is a Qal Imperative 2ms with a paragogic He: שָׁמְרָה. This is more than a request from the psalmist. It is an anguished prayer for divine deliverance when enemies are trying to kill him (86:14). Certainly one could argue that the psalmist is using a more polite form of address because he, a "poor and needy" (86:1) human being, is directing his imperatives to the Almighty God (function 1). It is also true that the psalmist has a personal investment or interest in the action that is being commanded (function 2). Indeed, he recognizes that his life is utterly dependent upon the saving action of his compassionate, gracious, loving, and faithful God (86:15). Only in God can his salvation be found.

Although exegetically it is dangerous to build conclusions on possibilities, our consideration of the possible functions of the paragogic He nevertheless reminds us of some important theological implications that might be overlooked in English translations of this imperative. First, that the paragogic He might suggest an appeal to one of higher authority implies that we should not order God around as though he were some sort of cosmic concierge who exists to fulfill our commands. Our appeals to him must proceed from an acknowledgment of the vast difference between us and God. But we *must* direct our appeals to him because he is the only one who will never disappoint or fail us. That leads to the second implication. Our appeals to God always involve a personal investment or interest on our part. At the same time our welfare is always the concern of our loving and faithful God. We come to him because we know that he alone is capable and knows how to provide what we need most. As the apostle Peter says to the church so many years later: "Cast all your anxiety on him because he cares for you" (1 Pet 5:7).

PARAGOGIC NUN

(Nun Paragogicum)

What It Looks Like

The paragogic Nun consists of a Nun attached to the end of a **verb** in Hebrew where it is not expected. In fact, the word "paragogic" means "to extend." So, the paragogic Nun "extends" the usual form of the verb. The paragogic Nun most frequently occurs at the end of **masculine, plural, Imperfect** verbs, though it also occurs at the end of **feminine singular** verbs. Consider the difference in form shown below between the **Qal**, Imperfect, 3mp form of שׁמע with and without the paragogic Nun attached to the end:

   without paragogic Nun with paragogic Nun

What It Does

The precise origin and meaning of the paragogic Nun is debated, so any statements regarding its function must remain tentative. The two most likely possibilities for its function are (1) that the paragogic Nun communicates additional force or emphasis, and (2) that the paragogic Nun signals that the verb to which it is attached is describing an action that is other than usual or expected.

An Exegetical Insight

The two possible functions of the paragogic Nun — signaling additional emphasis and signaling action that is other than usual or expected — are both present in all four occurrences of the paragogic Nun in Deuteronomy 4:28 (paragogic Nuns gray-shaded):

וַעֲבַדְתֶּם־שָׁם אֱלֹהִים מַעֲשֵׂה יְדֵי אָדָם עֵץ וָאֶבֶן
אֲשֶׁר לֹא־יִרְאוּן וְלֹא יִשְׁמְעוּן וְלֹא יֹאכְלוּן וְלֹא יְרִיחֻן

"There you will worship man-made gods of wood and stone,
which cannot see or hear or eat or smell."

The second line of this verse contains four verbs that end with paragogic Nuns. These verbs are situated within a divine reminder of the
stupidity of worshiping idols. They can't even perform these minimal bio-
logical functions, which the people who worshiped them would certainly
have expected them to be able to do. Thus, the paragogic Nuns might
very well be highlighting the contrast (function 2) between the minimum
expectations people might have for their idols and those idols' actual impo-
tence. It is also no doubt true that God is communicating through his
servant Moses with significant force (function 1). God knows his people's
susceptibility to idolatry and also that they would ultimately succumb to
the temptation. By listing the very basic things those idols cannot do, one
after the other, God hammers home the mindlessness of worshiping them.

Although we must be careful not to construct exegetical arguments
on grammatical features whose significance is not clearly understood, it is
legitimate to consider the two possible significations of the paragogic Nun
when we encounter it in the Hebrew text. The presence of the paragogic
Nuns may be reminding us that things aren't always what human beings
expect them to be, and that we often need to be forcefully reminded of
that fact.

PARTICIPLE, ACTIVE

What It Looks Like

The active Participle **conjugation** unsurprisingly only occurs in those **verb stem**s that have active voice (that is, **Qal**, **Hiphil**, and **Piel**). The forms of the active Participle are shown below for each of these verb stems. The boxes represent the **consonant**s of any three-consonant **root**:

		Active Participle Forms	
		Singular	Plural
Qal	Masculine	□ֹ□ֵ□	□ְ□ֹ□ים
	Feminine	ת □ֶ□ֹ□ or □ְ□ֹ□ה	□ְ□ֹ□ות
Hiphil	Masculine	מַ□ְ□ִי□	מַ□ְ□ִי□ים
	Feminine	מַ□ְ□ִי□ָה	מַ□ְ□ִי□ות
Piel	Masculine	מְ□ַ□ֵ□	מְ□ַ□ְ□ים
	Feminine	מְ□ַ□ֶ□ָה	מְ□ַ□ְ□ות

What It Does

The term "active" indicates that the action communicated by the verbal root transfers onto something else. For example, if I say "He is kicking the can," the word "kicking" is active because it indicates that what the subject

("He") is doing is being transferred onto something else ("the can").

The term "participle" indicates that the action itself is ongoing. So, the participle form usually ends in -ing. In a sentence, a participle functions in the same way that an **adjective** does. In fact, participles are *verbal* adjectives. That's why they take the same endings as adjectives. The only difference between participles and regular adjectives is that participles can take direct objects. That is, the action that the participle is communicating may transfer onto something else. Note the following sentences in which participles and (regular) adjectives are functioning similarly:

- Attributive adjective: The *good* woman is here.   The *offending* woman is here.

- Predicative adjective: The woman is *good*.   The woman is *offending* (others).

- Substantive adjective: Help the *poor* (people).   Help the *suffering* (people).

An Exegetical Insight

Understanding the nuance of ongoing action for the active participle deepens our understanding of biblical passages such as Psalm 121:4, where we can recognize a Qal Active Participle in the first part of the verse:

לֹא־יָנוּם וְלֹא יִישָׁן שׁוֹמֵר יִשְׂרָאֵל

"he who watches over Israel will neither slumber nor sleep"

The next-to-last word is the participle. It is difficult to capture the full sense of the participle in smooth English. As it stands, it could be wrongly understood to mean that the One *watching over* Israel will not sleep *in the future*, but he *is* sleeping now. Or, that the One *watching over* Israel will not sleep *now*, but perhaps he will *in the future*. Against these wrong understandings, the active participle communicates the fact that God's providential care is continuous, ongoing, uninterrupted. His eyes are on his people now and always. Who knew that the direct objects of God's fatherly care could have such comfort and assurance communicated to them by means of a Hebrew active participle!

PARTICIPLE, PASSIVE

What It Looks Like

The Passive Participle **conjugation** unsurprisingly only occurs in those **verb stem**s that have (or allow for) a passive voice (that is, **Qal**, **Niphal**, **Hophal**, and **Pual**). The **masculine singular** forms of the Passive Participle are shown below for each of these verb stems. The masculine **plural**, **feminine** singular, and feminine plural forms will have the corresponding **adjective** endings. The boxes represent the **consonant**s of any three-consonant **root**:

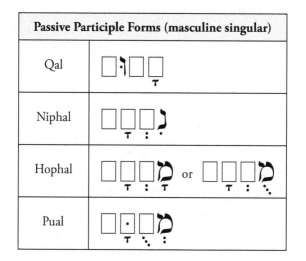

What It Does

The term "passive" indicates that the action communicated by the verbal root is done to the grammatical subject. For example, if I say "The book is being read," the phrase "being read" is passive because it indicates what is happening to the grammatical subject ("the book"). Note that the passive construction does not give the reader information regarding who is actually doing the reading; that is, who is the agent.

The term "participle" indicates that the action itself, or the effect of the action, is ongoing. So, the participle form usually ends in -ing. In a sentence, a participle functions in the same way that an adjective does. In fact, participles are *verbal* adjectives. That's why they take the same endings as adjectives.

An Exegetical Insight

A watershed moment in biblical history occurs in 1 Samuel 8. In this chapter, the Israelites ask for a king "such as all the other nations have" (8:5). In doing so, they were rejecting God as their king (8:7). Even after Samuel informs them of the great burden to them such a king would be (unlike their divine king), they still insist on having one. They subsequently end up with Saul, who begins his reign well, but slides steadily downward on a path of disobedience until he ends up a pathetic figure, futilely grasping at the kingdom while it passes over to David, the man after God's own heart.

Looking a little more closely at Saul's name in Hebrew reveals that it is a Qal passive participle (see the chart above): שָׁאוּל, from the root שׁאל, meaning "to ask." That is, Saul's very name communicates the fact that he is the one *being asked for* by the people. As Saul's leadership deteriorated, the people came to realize that what they had asked for was certainly not all they had hoped it would be. Having rejected God's leadership and demanding a king like all the other nations ultimately resulted in the death of "the asked for one" and the defeat of the nation at the hands of the Philistines. Perhaps rejecting God's leadership wasn't such a good idea. As the saying goes, "Beware of what you ask for, you just might get it." How much better to submit to the leadership of the one who knows what we need before we even ask him (Matt 6:8).

PARTICLE

What It Looks Like

A Hebrew particle has no distinguishing features that enable us to differentiate it from other kinds of Hebrew words. It has no markers for **person**, gender, or number. One must either learn particles as vocabulary words or depend on Bible software or other Hebrew language resources for their identification.

What It Does

Grammarians often include within the category of particle **conjunctions**, **adverb**s, **preposition**s, **interjection**s, and other kinds of words that do not follow regular patterns or paradigms. However, because these other kinds of words are dealt with elsewhere in this resource, here particle refers to those words that don't easily fit within other English grammatical categories. Because of this lack of correspondence to recognized English categories, their function and meaning can only be determined from their use in specific contexts.

An Exegetical Insight

An example of the need to be attentive to context in order to determine the meaning and function of particles, and the exegetical benefit of doing so, can be seen by an examination of the use of the particle הִנֵּה. The old KJV consistently translated this particle as "behold." However, that this particle certainly indicates something else is evidenced by the many awkward translations that resulted. For example, in Genesis 27:1, when Isaac, who could no longer see, calls for his son Esau, Jacob deceptively steps forward and says (according to the KJV): "Behold, *here am* I" (הִנֵּנִי = הִנֵּה + the 1cs pronoun suffix). Notice that the KJV has put "here am" in italics to signal that it believed those words were not included in the original Hebrew. Also notice that it would be impossible for blind Isaac to "behold" *anything*! More contemporary translations recognize that instead of meaning "behold," the particle הִנֵּה often suggests immediacy of time or place. So, in the context of Genesis 27:1 described above, the particle הִנֵּה is indicating immediacy of *place* (that is, "here"). Consequently, the words that the KJV has placed in italics are the actual meaning of הִנֵּה in this context, and the word it has *not* placed in italics ("behold") is inappropriate in this context!

Another context where הִנֵּה suggests immediacy of time is Genesis 38:13. In this verse, Tamar is told, "הִנֵּה your father-in-law is on his way to Timnah to shear his sheep." This could hardly be something Tamar could "behold." Her father-in-law was already on his way! Rather, the context suggests that in this context, הִנֵּה means something like "right now" or "at this moment."

Consider how this more contextually informed appraisal of this particle deepens our understanding of Isaiah 40:9. Isaiah has been prophesying about God's coming judgment upon his people, but beginning in chapter 40 his tone changes. Here Isaiah's prophecy turns to the time after the judgment, when God will come not to bring judgment but to bring healing and restoration. God is coming with blessing, and his coming is therefore excitedly anticipated. When Isaiah prophetically sees that event break into human history, in verse 9 he tells us that he hears a messenger being told to announce "הִנֵּה your God!" In other words, the messenger is told to announce that God's coming with blessing is *right here, right now*! The new day of the Lord's favor has dawned. The New Testament explicates the meaning of the day Isaiah saw breaking forth in time and space. It makes clear that the immediacy of God's presence in blessing is found today in Jesus Christ, who is "God with us" (Matt 1:23) right here, right now.

PERFECT

(Suffix Conjugation, Sufformative Conjugation, QTL Conjugation)

What It Looks Like

A Perfect **verb** is recognized by means of the **consonant**s and **vowel**s (called "sufformatives" or "suffixes") that attach to the end of the three-consonant **root**. That's why this **conjugation** is also called the "suffor-mative" or "suffix" conjugation. The identifying features of the Perfect conjugation are shared by all of Hebrew's seven verb **stem**s. These are shown below, attached to boxes that represent the verbal root:

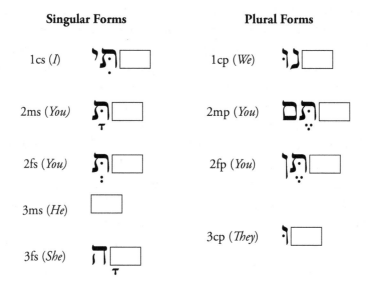

Singular Forms		Plural Forms	
1cs (*I*)	תִּי	1cp (*We*)	נוּ
2ms (*You*)	תָ	2mp (*You*)	תֶּם
2fs (*You*)	תְּ	2fp (*You*)	תֶּן
3ms (*He*)			
3fs (*She*)	הָ	3cp (*They*)	וּ

What It Does

The Perfect conjugation indicates that the action of the verb is viewed in its entirety, usually corresponding to completed action. Because the Hebrew verbal system is not based on time, as is the English verbal system, the completed action envisioned may be in the past, present, or future. However, most often the completed action of the Perfect conjugation is translated by the English past (he *ate*), perfect (he *has eaten*), or pluperfect (he *had eaten*). But verbs in the Perfect conjugation that indicate mental activity or disposition may also be translated in the present tense. Once again, context is the ultimate determining factor for which one of these translational options applies.

An Exegetical Insight

It is sometimes difficult to capture the sense of the Hebrew verb, which views the action in terms of its being complete or incomplete, by an English verb, which views the action in terms of the time in which it takes place. If we use the present tense in English, that leaves open the possibility that the verbal action being specified did not also take place in the past. For example, the statement "I like the taste of coffee" leaves open the possibility that such was not always the case. Knowing how the Hebrew verbal system works can help us to avoid such misinterpretations.

Consider, for example, Genesis 22:2, where God directs Abraham to sacrifice his son, Isaac. God tells Abraham, "Take your son, your only son, whom you love [אָהַבְתָּ] — Isaac — and go to the region of Moriah." We can tell by its ending (תָּ) that the indicated verb is in the Perfect conjugation, 2ms. But what is the best translation? Because it refers to mental activity or disposition (in this case, love), the verb may be translated in the present tense. But a verb in the Perfect conjugation may also be translated in the past, perfect, or pluperfect tense. So, does the verb in this case mean that Abraham "loves," "loved," "has loved," or "had loved" his son, Isaac? Unlike English, the Hebrew verb does not refer primarily to the time of the action, but to the perspective of the action. In this case, Abraham's love for Isaac is not restricted to a specific time. It is true that Abraham currently loves Isaac, but he has always loved Isaac and always will. It is the *fact* of Abraham's love that is the focus, not *when* it exists. That timeless love is hard to express in English, but rewarding to ponder when we consider God's love for us expressed in the sacrifice of Jesus Christ, the son whom He loves/loved/has loved.

PERSON

What It Looks Like

The features that enable one to identify "person" depend on whether the word is a **pronoun** or a **verb**. For a verb, the distinguishing features that represent person in the **Perfect, Imperfect, Imperative, Cohortative**, and **Jussive conjugation**s are found under those headings in this resource. For the forms of the **pronoun**s (**independent** and **suffixed**) for each person, see those headings in this resource.

What It Does

"Person" identifies the participants in the text, referred to as pronouns. The grammatical category of "person" is referred to as first, second, or third; and **singular** or **plural**. These are represented below:

	SINGULAR	**PLURAL**
FIRST PERSON:	I, me, my	we, us, our
SECOND PERSON:	you, your	you, your
THIRD PERSON:	He, she, it, his, him, hers, her, its	They, their, theirs, them

An Exegetical Insight

An example of the exegetical insights available simply by giving attention to the person(s) indicated in the text can be found in Isaiah's long song of praise in 26:7–21. Notice how many times in this passage the person changes. In verses 7 and 8, that Isaiah is representing his community is evident by his use of the words "we" and "our" in his address to God. The use of the first person plural reflects the fact that Isaiah is including himself in the larger community of God's people whose concerns he brings to the Lord. In the very next verses, however (26:9–11), Isaiah uses the first person singular, as evidenced by the phrase "my soul" (26:9). Isaiah's repeated use of the first person plural "us" in 26:12–15 indicates that he is once again including himself with the community. Then, in 26:16, the prophet separates himself from the community once again by using the third person plurals "they" and "them" to refer to his own people. Immediately after this verse, however, he rejoins the community by his repeated use of the first person plural "we" (26:17–18). The speaker is hard to determine in 26:19. Here Isaiah could very well be representing God directly by proclaiming a future resurrection. There seems to be a shift in the middle of 26:20 from an exhortation by God to a statement from the prophet. This is demonstrated by the first person, "*my* people," apparently spoken by God to his people, followed immediately by a reference to God in the third person ("*his* wrath") that continues into the next verse.

These changes in person are not the result of editorial clumsiness. Rather, they reflect a complex inner dynamic. The prophet represents God, God's people, and himself. The shift from first to second to third person is a textual manifestation of this multifaceted, multi-representational prophetic responsibility. Contemplating such changes in person both sharpens our understanding of the text and our appreciation for the difficult task of all who are called to represent God and his people.

PIEL

(Palel, Pealal, Pilel, Pilpel, Poel, and Polel)

What It Looks Like

The Piel **verb stem** usually has the following features that help one to identify it:

- A dot (a **Dagesh**) in the second **consonant** of the three-consonant **root** of the verb.
- If the Piel verb is in the **Imperfect conjugation**, there will be two vertical dots (a **Sheva**) under the consonant in front of the three-consonant root.
- Often, there will also be two horizontal dots (a Tsere) under the second consonant of the three-consonant root.

Here is an example of a Piel verb, with the three identifying features indicated:

Many variations of this basic pattern are possible (see subheading above) when the three-consonant root has a long middle **vowel**, contains a **guttural** consonant, or has the same consonant for its second and third root letters. These occasional variations in form, however, do not suggest departures from the basic nuances of the Piel, described below.

What It Does

The Piel verb stem can signify several things, but two are most common.

The first most common nuance of the Piel stem is "factitive." This simply means that the action of the verb is making something a fact; that is, it is causing something or someone to be in a state. For example, a verb in the **Qal** stem that means "to be unclean" would mean in the Piel stem: "to cause something or someone to be unclean/to be in an unclean state."

The second most common nuance of the Piel stem is "denominative." "Denominative" is a fancy way of saying that a verb has been made out of a **noun**. We do this in English, for example, when we say that we've "Googled" something. The proper noun "Google" has been made into a verb. So, we'd call that verb "denominative." A good Hebrew example would be the Piel verb in the example above. This verb comes from the noun דָּבָר, meaning "word." In Hebrew, the noun has been made into a verb by putting it into the Piel verb stem. So, יְדַבֵּר means "he *words* something," or, a little more smoothly, "he speaks."

An Exegetical Insight

How recognizing the Piel verb stem can enhance our understanding of the text can be seen by a comparison of Genesis 2:3 in the Hebrew and the English Bible. The Hebrew text of this verse contains the verb וַיְקַדֵּשׁ. You can see that it has all the features of the Piel verb stem that are described above. The three-consonant root of this verb is קדשׁ. This root has the basic meaning "to be holy." But when the verb has the features of the Piel verb stem, it unsurprisingly takes on one of the nuances of the Piel verb stem. In this case, it takes on the factitive nuance. So, we would translate this verb in this verse as "Then God blessed the seventh day and *put it into a state of holiness.*" That is, God caused the holiness of the seventh day *to be a fact.*

Consider how this deepens our understanding of the seventh day. God has made this day holy. He has made its holiness a fact. God calls upon his people to "remember" and "keep" the holiness of this day (Exod 20:8 and Deut 5:12). In essence, then, God calls upon his people to put this day into a state of holiness, just as he has. So, by keeping the seventh day, or Sabbath day, holy, God's people are imitating God himself.

PLURAL

What It Looks Like

Many grammatical categories in Hebrew have plurals. These include **noun**s, **adjective**s (including **participle**s), **verb**s, and **pronoun**s (both independent and suffixed). For details regarding the form of the plural in each of these, see the corresponding entries in this resource. Some rules of thumb, however, may be helpful:

- The ending ‎ים usually indicates a **masculine plural** noun or adjective.
- The ending ‎וֹת usually indicates a **feminine** plural noun or adjective.
- The ending ‎וּ usually indicates a masculine (or **common**) plural verb.
- The ending ‎נָה usually indicates a feminine plural verb.

What It Does

For most words, the designation "plural" indicates that there is more than one. A few nouns may have a "**dual**" ending in addition to the plural ending. (See the entry in this resource entitled Dual.) For those few nouns, the designation "plural" means that there are more than two.

An Exegetical Insight

One of the great ambiguities in the English language is the meaning of the word "you." It can be **singular** or plural. In Hebrew, this ambiguity does not exist. Pronouns and verbs have different forms for the "you" singular and the "you" plural. This greater clarity in Hebrew may have significant exegetical implications.

Consider, for example, God's command to Adam in the garden of Eden, before Eve was created: "You must not eat from the tree of the knowledge of good and evil" (Gen 2:17). The verb in this sentence is *singular*. Indeed, how could it be otherwise? No other human being had been created. Yet, even after Eve is created, God never repeats this command to her. The two human beings are in complete unity; what applies to one applies to both. When Eve is subsequently created and unites with Adam, we are told that they become a unity ("one flesh" — 2:24). Sin has not yet arrived to have its divisive effect. In the next chapter, however, the serpent diabolically and subtly drives a wedge into the unity of the first human couple by the very way he asks Eve his sinister question: "Did God really say, 'You must not eat from any tree in the garden'?" (3:1). The verb in this question is *plural*— oh so cleverly suggesting to Eve that the command was given to two individual agents who are free to decide independently of each other how they might respond to the divine command. That Eve fell for the serpent's ploy is evident in her response to the serpent, even before she reaches out her hand to take the forbidden fruit. She says, "God did say, 'You must not eat fruit from the tree ...'" (3:3). Eve uses a *plural* verb in her response to the serpent, indicating her acceptance of the fact that she may act independently of Adam. The unity of the first couple is broken already.

The devastating effects of sin's introduction are abundantly clear even in the English translations. But when one is able to examine the passage in the original Hebrew, even more details become apparent. Sin causes division. It causes division between human beings and God. And it causes division between one person and another — even between a husband and wife, perhaps suggested here as ingeniously as a change from a singular "you" to a plural one.

PREPOSITION

What It Looks Like

A Hebrew preposition has no distinguishing features that enable us to differentiate it from other kinds of words. It has no markers for **person**, gender, or number. One must either learn prepositions as vocabulary words or depend on Bible software or other Hebrew language resources for their identification. There are three different kinds of Hebrew prepositions:

1) Those that stand as independent words.
2) Those that may attach to the following word with a line (called a Maqqef).
   - עַל־ "on," "against," "concerning," etc. For example: עַל־סוּס "*on* a horse"
   - אֶל־ "to," "toward," etc. For example: אֶל־עִיר "*toward* a city"
   - מִן־ "from," "away from," "out of," etc. For example: מִן־עִיר "*from* a city"

3) *Inseparable* prepositions that attach directly to the front of the following word:
   - בְּ "in," "with," "by means of," etc. For example: בְּעִיר "*in* a city"
   - לְ "to," "for," etc. For example: לְאִישׁ "*to* a man"
   - כְּ "as," "according to," "like," "about," etc. For example: כְּסוּס "*like* a horse"

When a word begins with the **Definite Article**, the **consonant** of the inseparable preposition displaces the ה of the Definite Article. For example: הַמֶּלֶךְ (the king) + לְ becomes לַמֶּלֶךְ (for the king).

What It Does

A preposition in Hebrew performs the same function as a preposition in English. A preposition describes the relationship between the words in a sentence. For example, in the sentence "The book is *on* the desk," the italicized word is the preposition and it describes the relationship of the book to the desk.

An Exegetical Insight

In any language, prepositions are slippery things. For example, consider the different meanings for the English preposition "on" in the following sentences:

- The book was *on* the table.
- It was a book *on* the birds of North America.
- Ruining the book is *on* me.
- Now I don't think I can go *on*.

Of course, there are many more meanings for "on" that could be mentioned. The point is that it is not always easy to determine which one of the many possible meanings for a preposition is intended in the text. And yet any translation must pick just one. Being able to recognize the Hebrew preposition with which the translation is wrestling enables the reader to realize the full range of possibilities available.

An example of the exegetical difficulties surrounding the translation of a preposition can be observed with the phrase לְדָוִד in the superscription of many psalms. This form consists of the inseparable preposition לְ attached to the proper **noun** דָּוִד (David). But how should one translate the preposition? It could mean:

- *belonging to* David (that is, it is written *by* David)
- *for* David (that is, it is written to honor him, or is dedicated to him, or was commissioned by him)
- *about/concerning* David (that is, David is the subject matter)
- *in the style of* David

Other possibilities also exist. Thus, while knowledge of some Hebrew grammatical elements can clarify the meaning, knowledge of the wide semantic range of other grammatical elements, such as prepositions, can multiply possible meanings. This is one more reason to exercise great caution and give careful attention to context when forming exegetical conclusions.

PRONOUN, INDEPENDENT

What It Looks Like

The Hebrew independent pronoun has **person** (first, second, or third), gender (**masculine, feminine,** or **common**), and number (**singular** or **plural**). The different forms of the independent pronoun are presented below:

		SINGULAR	PLURAL
1st Person	COMMON	אָנֹכִי or אֲנִי	אֲנַ֫חְנוּ
2nd Person	MASCULINE	אַתָּה	אַתֶּם
	FEMININE	אַתְּ	אַתֵּ֫נָה
3rd Person	MASCULINE	הוּא	הֵ֫מָּה or הֵם
	FEMININE	הִיא	הֵ֫נָּה

Rare alternative forms also exist.

What It Does

The independent pronoun stands in place of a noun in the text. The noun it is standing in place of is called the "antecedent." For example, consider the following sentence: "The man bought a book and read it in two days." In this sentence, the pronoun "it" is standing in place of the noun "book." More technically, we could say that "book" is the antecedent of "it." Independent pronouns enable readers to keep track of who is doing what to whom.

An Exegetical Insight

Another use of independent pronouns is to indicate emphasis. Hebrew **verb**s contain pronouns within them, so they do not require independent pronouns as English verbs do. For example, the Hebrew verb שָׁמַר can be translated as "*he* guarded." The pronoun "he" comes installed from the factory — built right into the verb — so no extra independent pronoun needs to be used. Sometimes, however, we *do* encounter the use of independent pronouns in situations such as these. In these cases, the presence of this grammatical element where it is not required indicates a special emphasis. In English we often use italics, bold text, or some other mechanical means to indicate such emphasis. Such devices are, unfortunately, unavailable to translators. Consequently, this obvious emphasis in the Hebrew text is not always obvious in English translations.

Consider, for example, the beautiful contrast David is making in Psalm 59:14 – 16 (15 – 17 in Hebrew). In verses 14 – 15, David describes the noises made by those who slander him as "snarling like dogs" (v. 14). He goes on to say that they "howl if not satisfied" (v. 15). Unlike the verbal effluent of such people, who grumble and wail when they don't get what they want, David says to God in verse 16, "I will sing of your strength" (אֲנִי אָשִׁיר עֻזֶּךָ). Notice that the first word in this sentence is the first person singular independent pronoun "I" (אֲנִי). The following verb is a **Qal Imperfect** 1cs, which already includes the pronoun sense within it. So, the use of a separate 1cs pronoun is not necessary. Preceding this verb with the independent pronoun is therefore communicating an emphasis. David is emphasizing the difference between the focus of his heart and words and those of his enemies. It is as though David were saying to God, "No matter what they say about me, I will keep my worshipful attention on you!" Many believers today face similar social resistance, and David's words encourage a similar response: "But *I* will sing of your strength!"

PRONOUN, RELATIVE

What It Looks Like

The Hebrew relative pronoun has no **person**, gender, or number. It has a single form:

What It Does

The relative pronoun is translated into English as "who," "which," or "that." It is used to introduce clauses that modify a **noun**. That is, the clause that the relative pronoun introduces acts like one large **adjective**. In the following examples, all the clauses that follow the noun are describing that noun. They are therefore introduced by the relative pronoun and are called "relative clauses." These relative clauses, introduced by the relative pronoun, have been placed in italics for easy identification.

- the trees of Mamre, *which are at Hebron*
  (בְּאֵלֹנֵי מַמְרֵא אֲשֶׁר בְּחֶבְרוֹן)—Gen 13:18)
- the word *that he commanded you* (הַדָּבָר אֲשֶׁר צִוָּה אֶתְכֶם)—Josh 1:13)
- the peoples *who were around them* (הָעַמִּים אֲשֶׁר סְבִיבוֹתֵיהֶם—Judg 2:12)

Often for a smoother English translation, the relative pronoun is not translated. For example, the Scripture passages above could be translated as:

- the trees of Mamre at Hebron
- the word he commanded you
- the peoples around them

What is gained in smoothness by eliding the relative pronoun may, however, come at the expense of literary or rhetorical effect.

An Exegetical Insight

An example of an exegetical insight afforded by the repeated use of the relative pronoun is found in Jeremiah 7:14. In this context, Jeremiah is confronting his fellow Judahites who believe they can continue to sin and yet find refuge in the temple. After all, God would never destroy his own house! Through his prophet Jeremiah, God delivers the crushing news that his temple will not be a safe haven for those who rebel against him. He will, in fact, destroy it along with their false sense of security. To deliver this news clearly and powerfully, God repeatedly uses relative clauses to describe the temple. He calls it:

- the house *that bears my Name*
- the temple [*that*] *you trust in*
- the place [*that*] *I gave to you and your ancestors*

Their trust in the inviolability of the temple is understandable. One can see from the above list of relative clauses that the people's trust is sandwiched between reasons for that trust that are rooted in God himself. How inconceivable the destruction of the temple must have been for them! Indeed, God tells Jeremiah that they won't believe him regarding this (7:27)—even though he leaves no doubt by hammering away at their misplaced trust with three relative clauses. But the reason for the destruction of the seemingly impregnable temple, and those who seek refuge within it, also contains a relative clause:

זֶה הַגּוֹי אֲשֶׁר לוֹא־שָׁמְעוּ בְּקוֹל יְהוָה אֱלֹהָיו

This is the nation that has not obeyed the LORD its God (7:28).

The relationship between the descriptions of the temple, and the judgment that follows from trust in such descriptions instead of obedience to the God who inhabits the temple, is much clearer when one gives careful attention to the relative pronoun and the clauses it introduces.

PRONOUN, SUFFIX

(Pronominal Suffix, Suffix)

What It Looks Like

The Hebrew pronoun (or pronominal) suffix has a different form for **person**, gender, and number. Also, the forms of the pronoun suffixes attached to **verb**s differ slightly from those attached to **noun**s. This variety of forms is indicated in the chart below:

ATTACHED TO:	A SINGULAR NOUN	A PLURAL NOUN	A VERB
1cs (my, me)	נִי or יָ	יַ	נִי, נִי, or נִי
2ms (your, you)	ךָ	יךָ	ךָ or ךָ
2fs (your, you)	ךְ	יִךְ	ךְ or ךְ
3ms (his, he)	וֹ, הוּ, or הֹ	יו or יהוּ	נּוּ, הוּ, וֹ, or נּוּ
3fs (her, she)	הָ or הָ	יהָ	הָ, הָ, or נּהָ
1cp (our, us)	נוּ	ינוּ	נּוּ, נוּ, or נּוּ
2mp (your, you)	כֶם	יכֶם	כֶם
2fp (your, you)	כֶן	יכֶן	כֶן
3mp (their, they)	הֶם or ם	יהֶם	ם, הֶם, or מוֹ
3fp (their, they)	הֶן or ן	יהֶן	הֶן or ן

A pronoun suffix may also be attached to a **preposition**, the **definite direct object marker**, and some **particle**s.

What It Does

A pronoun suffix attached to a noun indicates possession (for example, "*my* house"). The pronoun suffix attached to a verb or preposition indicates the object of that verb or preposition (for example, "he built *it* for *me*").

An Exegetical Insight

Recognizing pronoun suffixes at times clarifies our understanding of the English translation, and at times raises alternative possibilities. Consider, for example, the opening words of the book of Malachi: "A prophecy: The word of the LORD to Israel through Malachi" (Mal 1:1). The word translated "Malachi" (מַלְאָכִי) is the noun "messenger" (מַלְאָךְ) with a 1cs pronoun suffix (׳ , "my") attached. This raises the question whether "Malachi" is a proper noun with this meaning or simply means "my messenger." That is, is God speaking through an unnamed prophet in this last book of the Old Testament before the One who is the fulfillment of prophecy and the prophetic office arrives, or is God speaking through a specific individual named Malachi, who is never again mentioned in this book, or indeed in the entire Bible?

The Septuagint (the Greek translation of the Old Testament) renders the term "Malachi" as ἀγγέλου αὐτοῦ (that is, "his messenger"), apparently supporting the idea that the term is a common noun with a pronoun suffix. However, if that were the case, it would be the only occurrence in the Bible of an anonymous prophetic book. Nevertheless, there might be some point being made in using an unspecified prophetic messenger. Such an unspecified messenger is referred to in Malachi 3:1 (מַלְאָכִי — "my messenger"). In the New Testament, Jesus makes it clear that this general designation refers to John the Baptist (Matt 11:7 – 10), although the people of Jesus' day did not readily make that connection. Perhaps the specific identification of the general reference to "my messenger" in Malachi 1:1, which is followed by a statement of God's relentless love ("I have loved you") in the next verse, ultimately is found in the incarnation of God's love that comes in the next book. But the matter remains undecided.

PUAL

(Poal, Polal, Polpal, and Pulal)

What It Looks Like

The Pual **verb stem** occurs most frequently in the **Perfect, Imperfect**, and **Participle conjugation**s. It has several characteristic features in these conjugations that enable one to differentiate the Pual from other Hebrew verb stems:

- A dot (a **Dagesh**) in the second **consonant** of the three-consonant **root** of the verb.
- In the **Imperfect** conjugation, there will be two vertical dots (a **Sheva**) under the consonant in front of the three-consonant root (that is, the preformative consonant).
- A Qibbuts under the first consonant of the three-consonant root.
- In the **Participle** conjugation, the three-consonant root will be preceded by מְ.

Consider the following example of a Pual Imperfect verb (3ms) with its identifying features indicated:

Dagesh   Qibbuts   Sheva

Many variations of this basic pattern are possible (see subheading above) when the three-consonant root has a long middle vowel, contains a **guttural** consonant, or has the same consonant for its second and third root letters. These occasional variations in form, however, do not suggest departures from the basic nuances of the Pual, described below.

What It Does

The Pual verb stem is the passive of the **Piel** verb stem. The Piel verb stem is used (1) to suggest causing (someone or something) to be in a certain state, or (2) to make a verb out of a **noun**. So, the Pual would signify the passive of one of these two nuances.

An Exegetical Insight

In Psalm 18:3 [Hebrew 18:4] we encounter a form of the Pual that gives us an insight into the character of God. In Hebrew, the first part of this verse is only three words: מְהֻלָּל אֶקְרָא יְהוָה. It takes many more words to translate this smoothly into English: "I called to the LORD, who is worthy of praise." The first word is a Pual Participle (ms) from the three-consonant root הלל. It has all the features of a Pual described above. Participles are **adjectives** (see the entry in this resource entitled Adjective) and, like English adjectives, can stand alone as nouns. In this verse, the Pual Participle is acting like a noun. In the Piel, the root הלל has the general meaning "to praise" or, more awkwardly, "to put into the state of being praised." In the Pual, which is the passive of the Piel, the Participle form would mean "being praised" or "being put into the state of being praised." However, in this verse, the Pual Participle is standing as a noun paralleling "the LORD" (יְהוָה). We could translate it, therefore, as something like "The Being Praised One" or "The One Who Is in the State of Being Praised." God is not just praiseworthy; he is actually continually praised! Coming into his presence, then, requires that we, too, come with praise to add to that which already surrounds him. Indeed, the apostle Peter tells us that we exist as God's chosen people for this very reason — to declare his praise (1 Pet 2:9). All his works bring God praise. The only question is whether we will choose to join in.

QAL

What It Looks Like

The Qal **verb stem** is recognized by the *lack* of distinctive features that characterize the other verb stems. In fact, the word "Qal" means "light" or "simple." It is the foundational or basic stem from which all the other verb stems are formed (or "derived"). For the distinctive features of the other verb stems, see the entries in this resource entitled **Niphal**, **Hiphil**, **Hophal**, **Piel**, **Pual**, and **Hitpael**.

What It Does

A verb in the Qal stem communicates simple action with an active voice.

"Simple" action means that the action does not cause another action or state, does not reflect back on the subject of the verb, and is not reciprocated. The action is straightforward. For example, שָׁמַר ("he guarded") is a Qal verb and so communicates simple action.

"Active voice" means that the subject of the verb is doing or actively engaged in the action that the verb is specifying.

Within these broad parameters, a Qal verb can communicate a wide variety of actions and states.

An Exegetical Insight

Because the Qal stem is the base or foundational stem from which the six other Hebrew verb stems are derived, understanding the meaning of a verb in the Qal stem can contribute to the understanding of a verb with the same three-**consonant root** in one of those other verb stems.

For example, the meaning of the three-consonant root למד in the Qal verb stem is "to learn." Its meaning in the Piel verb stem is usually given as "to teach." But we have a deeper understanding of what is meant by "teach" when we appreciate the relationship of the Qal verb stem to the Piel verb stem. One of the nuances of the Piel verb stem is that it causes the meaning of the three-consonant root in the Qal stem to become a fact. In this case, then, what the three-consonant root in the Piel verb stem is communicating is that *learning* has been made a fact. In other words, learning has taken place; it has become a reality. That is the sense of "to teach" that is meant — not lecture coherency, rhetorical power, or multimedia presentations. Those accoutrements of teaching may be effective, but they are potential means to learning and do not ensure that the desired learning has actually become a reality.

Consider how knowing the meaning of למד in the Qal verb stem thus deepens our understanding of its use in the Piel verb stem in Psalm 25:4–5, for example. In these verses, David twice implores the Lord to "teach" him:

> Show me your ways, LORD,
>   teach [למד — Piel verb stem] me your paths,
> Guide me in your truth and teach [למד — Piel verb stem] me,
>   for you are God my Savior
>   and my hope is in you all day long.

Appreciating how the meaning of the Piel verb stem derives from the meaning of the Qal verb stem enables us to comprehend the true nature of David's request. He is expressing his desire to grow in his understanding and experience of the Lord and the life that he offers. David is not necessarily looking for additions to his files on sermons or lectures or books for his library. Indeed, we've all been in situations where a whole lot of "teaching" was taking place, but not much learning was happening. David is not looking for that kind of teaching to take place. He *is* primarily looking for learning, growth, and progress in his spiritual journey to take place. May our prayer, like David's, not be that God "teaches" (Qal verb stem) us, but that God causes us to learn (Piel verb stem).

ROOT

What It Looks Like

The consonantal root of a Hebrew word can be located by removing all its **vowel**s, **Dagesh**es, prefixes, **suffix**es, and infixes (additions inside a word). If the word is a **verb**, all conjugational additions must be removed as well. What remains after all these have been removed is the root of the word. For example, in 2 Samuel 20:2, we encounter the ungainly בְּמַלְכָּם. To determine the root, we remove the inseparable **preposition** בְּ at the front and the 3mp **pronoun** suffix ם at the end. Then, after removing the vowels and the Dagesh, we are left with the root מ–ל–כ.

What It Does

In Hebrew, as in all Semitic languages, words are constructed around three-**consonant** roots. The root informs the reader or hearer of the basic meaning of the word that is being nuanced by all of its additional elements, such as those associated with **stem**s, **conjugation**s, prefixes, suffixes, and infixes.

For example, the three-consonant root uncovered above, מ–ל–כ, has a basic meaning of "rule," or "reign." Many different nuances of this basic idea can be expressed by means of additions to the end, beginning, or inside of this root. Just a few of these are indicated below:

- מֶלֶךְ   "king"
- מַלְכָּה   "queen"
- מֹלֵךְ   "reigning"
- מָלַךְ   "he reigned"
- יִמְלֹךְ   "he reigns/will reign"
- הִמְלִיךְ   "he made [someone] king"
- מַלְכוּת   "kingdom/realm"

An Exegetical Insight

Sometimes words with the same three-consonant root will have different meanings. An example of such a homonym in English is the word "rose": The two different meanings of this word are apparent in the sentence, "The rose rose from the ground."

Many times in biblical Hebrew, the author will play on such different meanings of the same three-consonant root in order to make his point. The fact that the author is using a homonym for his rhetorical purposes is obvious in Hebrew but usually invisible in English translations.

Consider, for example, the first vision Jeremiah records, in which he reports seeing "the branch of an almond tree" (Jer 1:11). The Hebrew word for "almond tree" is שָׁקֵד. Its root is שׁ–ק–ד. In an apparent non-sequitur, the Lord tells Jeremiah in the next verse: "You have seen correctly, for I am watching to see that my word is fulfilled." What, one may understandably ask, does this pronouncement by the Lord have to do with an almond tree? The missing link in English is visible in the Hebrew. The word translated as "watching" is שֹׁקֵד, with the same three-consonant root as "almond tree" (שׁ–ק–ד). By means of these identical roots God has made a connection between the presence of the almond tree and his watching over, or ensuring, the fulfillment of his word. The one has become the sign of the other—a sign that becomes comprehensible when we recognize the identical roots of the two words. Just one more reason to root for roots.

SINGULAR

What It Looks Like

Many grammatical categories in Hebrew have singular forms. These include **noun**s, **adjective**s (including **participle**s), **verb**s, and **pronoun**s (both independent and suffixed). For details regarding the form of the singular in each of these, see the corresponding entries in this resource. A couple rules of thumb, however, may be helpful:

- A **masculine** singular is usually indicated by the absence of an ending on the **root** form.
- A **feminine** singular is usually indicated by one of the following endings: הָ, תָ, תֶ, וּת, or תְ.

What It Does

As in English, the designation "singular" indicates that the word is referring to one of something or is governed by a single agent.

An Exegetical Insight

Something as seemingly pedestrian as the grammatical category of singular can still yield exegetical insights. An example of such an available insight is located in the story of Joseph in the book of Genesis.

At one point during his wearisome ordeal as a slave in Egypt, Joseph is unexpectedly summoned from the dungeon by Pharaoh himself. Genesis 41 recounts the details. During Joseph's incarceration, Pharaoh has had dreams that "all the magicians and wise men of Egypt" were unable to explain for him (41:8). At his wits' end, and at the suggestion of his cup-bearer who had up to this point neglected his obligation to help Joseph, Pharaoh deigns to consult the imprisoned Hebrew slave.

Throughout the next verses, the narrator skillfully plays with the use of the singular and the **plural** forms to hint at how the principal characters understand the relationship between the dreams Pharaoh has had. Is the reader supposed to regard Pharaoh's dreams as plural, or rather as a singular dream in two iterations? The narrator already signals the existing confusion on this point on the part of the narrative's characters by the way he alternates between the singular and plural in verse 8: "Pharaoh told them his dream [singular in Hebrew], but no one could interpret them [plural in Hebrew] for him." The magicians and wise men of Egypt have no clue regarding the meaning of the dream(s) or that the dream is a unity. In contrast, the singular meaning of the seemingly plural dreams is highlighted by Joseph by means of his emphatic repetition: חֲלוֹם אֶחָד הוּא ("the dream [singular in Hebrew] … is a unity") in 41:25–26.

The narrator has called attention to the difference and superiority of Joseph over against the Egyptians—contrary to what their physical situations might suggest. The singular representative of the true God has put to shame the plural wise men of the Egyptian court, just as the singular God would put to shame the plural gods of the Egyptians in the next book. By the skillful interplay of singular and plural forms, the author of Genesis has underscored and deepened the message of the narrative for those who can access and benefit from the Hebrew in which it is communicated.

STEM

What It Looks Like

The distinguishing features of the seven **verb** stems are explained in the entries in this resource entitled **Qal**, **Niphal**, **Hiphil**, **Hophal**, **Piel**, **Pual**, and **Hitpael**. Identifying the presence of these distinguishing features is necessary in order to determine a verb's stem, and the possible implications of that stem, so that the appropriate contextually nuanced translation of the verbal idea can be discerned.

What It Does

The stem of a verb indicates the *kind* of action being communicated by the three-**consonant root**. The kinds of action communicated by the verbal stem include active, passive, reflexive, causative, declarative, and factitive.

An Exegetical Insight

It is exegetically helpful not only to know the meaning of the verbal root, but also to know how that meaning is nuanced by the kind of action the verbal stem specifies. There is a great difference, for example, between saying "I did something" (simple, active action) and "I caused someone else to do something" (causative action). In the first case, I alone am responsible for the action. In the second case, I have exerted my influence over someone else. So, even though the subject of the verb (I) and the verbal idea (doing) are the same in both cases, the kind of action is quite different. Thus, attention to the verb stem is critical for accurate exegesis.

An example of how attention to the verb stem can yield exegetical fruit is found in Nahum 2:6–8 (2:7–9 in Hebrew), in God's judgment against Nineveh. This is one of the most verb stem-rich contexts in all of the Old Testament. In the course of only three verses, six of the seven Hebrew verb stems are represented. It is as though God is using almost every verb stem to communicate the fact that his judgment against Nineveh will involve every kind of action possible (italics added):

⁶The river gates *are thrown open* [Niphal stem]
    and the palace *collapses* [Niphal stem].
⁷It *is decreed* [Hophal stem] that Nineveh
    be exiled [Pual stem] and *carried away* [Hophal stem].
 Her female slaves *moan* [Piel stem] like doves
    and *beat* [Poel stem] on their breasts.
⁸Nineveh is like a pool
    whose water *is draining away* [Qal stem].
 "*Stop! Stop!*" [Qal stem] they cry,
    but no one *turns back* [Hiphil stem].

In other words, there is no escape for Nineveh from God's judgment. It is coming at them in every kind of way. The judgment is active, passive, reflexive, causative, declarative, and factitive—a fact communicated by the multiplicity of verb stems employed to describe it.

Reading only the English text of these verses certainly communicates clearly the coming downfall of Nineveh. But reading this passage in Hebrew, and recognizing the multiple verb stems in which the narrator has taken pains to describe Nineveh's end, enables the reader to grasp more deeply the breadth, the certainty, the awesomeness, and the awfulness of that end—to realize more fully, in other words, what a dreadful thing it is to fall into the hands of the living God (Heb 10:31). That realization should prompt us to appreciate more fully the good news contrastively proclaimed just prior to these verses, in 1:15 (2:1 in Hebrew).

VERB

What It Looks Like

Several elements contribute to the appearance of a verb in the Hebrew text. The verb is built upon a three-**consonant root**, which will have specific features characteristic of the particular **stem** in which that verb occurs. The verb also has the requisite conjugational elements of **person**, gender, and number. The verb may also have a **pronoun suffix**. Finally, the verb may have a **Waw Consecutive**, **conjunction**, or **interrogative He** at the beginning. Thus, the possible forms of a verb are quite numerous. The verb may usually be readily spotted, however, by its regular place at the very beginning of the clause.

What It Does

The verb indicates an action or state of being. Moreover, the form of the Hebrew verb indicates the *kind* and direction of the action (active, passive, reflexive, causative, declarative, or factitive). The inflection of the verb within its conjugation informs the reader of the person, gender, and number of the subject of the verb. Thus, verbs are critical to understanding *who* is doing *what* in the text.

An Exegetical Insight

The Hebrew Bible can be described as "verb-forward." This is true both conceptually and graphically. The regular pattern of Hebrew narrative is to place the verb at the beginning of the clause, and the verbs also serve as conceptual anchor points for navigating the text. The exegete must therefore give careful attention to Hebrew verbs in order to delve deeper into the treasures of biblical literature.

One insight that surfaces from a closer examination of the careful literary use of a specific verb is found in the prophecy of Nahum. In Nahum 1:8, the prophet gives God's people the good news that he would bring to an end those who had cruelly oppressed them, and indeed the whole ancient Near Eastern world. Their downfall is described symbolically as resulting from "an overwhelming flood." The verbal form translated as "overwhelming" is עֹבֵר — a Qal Active **Participle** ms from the root ע–ב–ר.

Forming a bookend with this announcement is the occurrence of this same verb at the very end of the book. In the last verse of Nahum's prophecy (3:19), the king of Assyria is told that this judgment will happen to his nation, and that all who hear about it will rejoice over it, because "upon whom has not come your unceasing evil?" (ESV) The word "come" in this verse is once again the verb ע–ב–ר (עָבְרָה). Though the connection is not visible in English, the narrator has used this one verb to tie together action and consequence. Because Assyria's cruelty has "passed over" everyone else, they would experience God's flood of judgment "passing over" them. The judgment fits the crime.

This is only one of many examples of how identifying the verbs in the Hebrew text and reflecting on their significance enables the exegete to enter more fully into the literary world of the biblical author and appreciate more fully the verbal brush strokes that contribute to his narrative artistry.

WAW CONSECUTIVE

(Waw Conversive)

What It Looks Like

There are two kinds of Waw Consecutives in Hebrew, one for the **Perfect conjugation** and one for the **Imperfect** conjugation. The Waw Consecutive only occurs as a form attached to one of these two conjugations.

The Waw Consecutive for the Perfect conjugation looks just like the regular conjunction attached directly to the front of the **verb**. Consider the following **Qal** Perfect verb with the Waw Consecutive attached:

Waw Consecutive

Even though the Waw Consecutive attached to the Perfect conjugation and the regular conjunction look the same, you can tell you have a Waw Consecutive attached to the Perfect conjugation when the *preceding* verb is something other than another verb in the Perfect conjugation.

The Waw Consecutive for the Imperfect conjugation consists of a Waw, Patakh, and a dot (a **Dagesh**) in the following **consonant**. Note: the Dagesh may be missing if the consonant in which it would normally be inserted is followed by a **Sheva**. Consider the following Qal Imperfect verb with the Waw Consecutive attached:

Waw Consecutive

What It Does

The Waw Consecutive, whether attached to a Perfect or an Imperfect verb, signifies that the action of the verb to which it is attached *logically* or *chronologically follows* the previous action. This is where the term "Waw Consecutive" comes from. The action this feature marks is *consecutive* action — action that occurs in a sequence.

The Waw Consecutive is also called the Waw Conversive because in addition to marking consecutive action, it will also "convert" the time (or aspect) of the verb to which it is attached.

- When the Waw Consecutive/Waw Conversive is attached to a verb in the Imperfect conjugation, it converts the action of the verb to that of the Perfect conjugation.

- When the Waw Consecutive/Waw Conversive is attached to a verb in the Perfect conjugation, it converts the action of the verb to that of whatever verb comes before it.

An Exegetical Insight

Consider the first two statements of Genesis 39:2 in both the Hebrew and the English Bible. There we read, "The LORD was with Joseph" and that "he [that is, Joseph] prospered." The verb in the second statement has a Waw Consecutive attached to it. Consider how knowing this gives us new insight into this verse. We now recognize that we shouldn't understand these two statements as two unrelated, positive features of Joseph's life. (See, for example, the translation of the KJV.) Rather, we should understand (and translate) the second statement as *logically* following the first: "The Lord was with Joseph *and as a consequence* he prospered." The Lord's presence is powerfully fruitful!

APPENDICES

THE HEBREW CONSONANTS

(Syllables indicated in bold and caps are stressed in pronunciation.)

The Printed Form of the Consonant	The Name of the Consonant (And How to Pronounce the Name)	The Sound of the Consonant	How the Hebrew Consonant Is Indicated by English Letters or Symbols (Transliteration)
א	Alef (**AH**-lef)	A catch in your throat—like the catch between the "o" in "so" and the "o" in "over" in the phrase "so over." We don't indicate this "catch" or interruption in English, but Hebrew indicates it with the א.	' (Similar in shape and placement to an apostrophe, or a superscript, backwards "c," or nothing)
ב	Bet (**BAYT**)	It depends. If there is a dot in the ב (בּ), it sounds like a "b." If there is no dot in the ב, it sounds like a "v."	With a dot inside: b With no dot inside: b or v
ג	Gimel (**GIM**-el)	This is another consonant that may or may not have a dot inside. Either way, however, it sounds like a "g."	With a dot inside: g With no dot inside: $\bar{g}$ or gh

	Name	Description	Pronunciation
ר	Dalet (**DAH**-let)	This is another consonant that may or may not have a dot inside. Either way, however, it sounds like a "d."	With a dot inside: d With no dot inside: $\underline{d}$ or dh
ה	He (**HAY**)	Like an "h"	h
ו	Waw (**VAHV**)	Like a "v"	w or v
ז	Zayin (**ZAH**-yin)	Like a "z"	z
ח	Khet (**KHET**)	This is a toughie because we don't have any letter in English that sounds like this. We do make the sound of this consonant when we really stress the end of "ick." This letter also sounds like the "ch" at the end of the German word "ach" (if that helps).	$\d{h}$, $\d{h}$, or kh
ט	Tet (**TET**)	Like a "t"	$\d{t}$ or t
י	Yod (**YOHD**)	Like a "y"	y

Letter	Description	Transliteration
כ Kaf (**KAHF**) (which appears as ך at the end of words)	This is another consonant that may or may not have a dot inside. If there is a dot in the כ (כּ), it sounds like a "k." If there is no dot in the כ, it sounds similar to the ח (see above).	With a dot inside: *k* With no dot inside: *k* or *kh*
ל Lamed (**LAH**-med)	Like an "l"	*l*
מ Mem (**MAYM**) (which appears as ם at the end of words)	Like an "m"	*m*
נ Nun (**NOON**) (which appears as ן at the end of words)	Like an "n"	*n*
ס Samek (**SAH**-mek)	Like an "s"	*s*
ע Ayin (**AH**-yin)	Like the א described above	ʿ (a backwards Alef—see above) or nothing

Hebrew	Name	Description	Sound
פ (which appears as ף at the end of words)	Pe (**PAY**)	This is another consonant that may or may not have a dot inside. If there is a dot in the פ (פּ), it sounds like a "p." If there is no dot in the פ, it sounds like an "f."	With a dot inside: *p* With no dot inside: *p̄* or *f*
צ (which appears as ץ at the end of words)	Tsade (**TSAH**-day)	Like the combination of the sounds in "ts"	*ṣ* or *ts*
ק	Qof (**KOHF**)	Like a "k"	*q*
ר	Resh (**RAYSH**)	Like an "r"	*r*
שׂ	Sin (**SEEN**)	Like an "s"	*ś* or *s*
שׁ	Shin (**SHEEN**)	Like an "sh"	*š* or *sh*
ת	Tav (**TAHV**)	This is another consonant that may or may not have a dot inside. Either way, however, it sounds like a "t."	With a dot inside: *t* With no dot inside: *ṯ* or *th*

THE HEBREW VOWELS

Vowel	Length	Printed Form of the Vowel (after ע)	Name of the Vowel (and How to Pronounce It)	Sound of the Vowel	How the Hebrew Vowel Is Indicated by English (Transliteration) Letters or Symbols
A	Long	עָ or עָה (at the end of words)	Qamets (KAH-mets) or Qa-mets He (KAH-mets HAY)	Like the "a" in "father"	*ā* or *â* or *ah* or *a*
A	Short	עַ	Patakh (PAH-takh)	Like the "a" in "father"	*a*
E	Long	עֵ or עֵי	Tsere (TSAY-ray) or Tsere Yod (TSAY-ray YOHD)	Like the "ay" in "say"	*ē* or *ê* or *e*
E	Short	עֶ	Segol (se-GOHL)	Like the "e" in "bed"	*e*
I	Long	עִי	Hireq Yod (HEER-ek YOHD)	Like the "ee" in "seen"	*î* or *i*
I	Short	עִ	Hireq (HEER-ek)	Like the "i" in "sin"	*i*
O	Long	עֹ or עוֹ	Holem (KHOHL-em) or Full Holem (KHOHL-em)	Like the "oa" in "boat"	*ō* or *ô* or *o*
O	Short	עָ	Qamets Khatuf (KAH-mets Khah-TOOF)	Like the "o" in "cot"	*o*
U	Long	עוּ	Shureq (SHOO-rek)	Like the "oo" in "moo"	*û* or *u*
U	Short	עֻ	Qibbuts (Kib-BOOTS)	Like the "oo" in "book"	*u*

THE GUTTURAL CONSONANTS

There are four **consonants** in Hebrew that are further classified as *guttural* consonants. These consonants are א, ה, ח, and ע. Guttural consonants are so called because they are all formed in the throat, and *guttur* is the Latin word for throat. Other than their pronunciation, what sets these four consonants apart from all the rest are three characteristic features:

1) Guttural consonants will *never* take a Dagesh. (For a discussion regarding the kinds and functions of **Dageshes**, see the Appendix below.) When normal grammatical rules would require a Dagesh in a guttural consonant, one of two alternatives are followed, and there is no rule for determining which one it will be:

   • The Dagesh will not be written in the guttural consonant, but the word will behave as though it were. This is called a *virtual* Dagesh. For example, compare the following two **verbs** with the same **person**, gender, number, **stem**, and **conjugation**:

   The **vowels** of the two verbs are exactly the same. The verb on the left, however, is missing the Dagesh in its second **root** consonant (ח) because it is a guttural consonant.

   • The vowel immediately before the guttural consonant will be lengthened to compensate for not being able to put the Dagesh in the guttural consonant. This is called *compensatory lengthening*. Again, compare the following two verbs with the same person, gender, number, stem, and conjugation to observe the difference the guttural consonant makes:

In this case, the verb on the left has a guttural consonant (א) corresponding to the consonant of the verb on the right that contains a Dagesh (ב). So, in order to *compensate*, what would be a Patakh (a short "a" vowel) in front of the guttural consonant has lengthened to a Qamets (a long "a" vowel).

2) If the form and accent of a word require the guttural consonant to have a vocal **Sheva**, it will have a compound Sheva instead of a normal Sheva. (See the end of the Appendix entitled Shevas for a discussion regarding these kinds of Shevas.) Compare the form of the following two **masculine**, **plural noun**s:

עֲבָדִים   דְּבָרִים

The two nouns have almost identical vowels. The only difference is the kind of Sheva under the first consonant. The noun on the left begins with a non-guttural consonant (ד) and has a regular vocal Sheva under that consonant. However, because the noun on the right begins with a guttural consonant (ע), it has a compound Sheva under that consonant.

3) Guttural consonants prefer to surround themselves with "a" vowels. Because the "a" vowels are also formed at the back of the throat where guttural consonants are formed, it is easier for Hebrew speakers to use "a" vowels instead of other vowels in the vicinity of guttural consonants. Compare the following two verbs with the same person, gender, number, stem, and conjugation to see how the verb on the right has changed the Holem of the regular vowel pattern (indicated by the verb on the left) to an "a" vowel (a Patakh) due to the presence of the guttural consonant ע:

SYLLABLES

In any language, words are made up of syllables. Syllables are language-appropriate combinations of **vowels** and **consonants**. English has a wide variety of acceptable syllables. Consider the range of syllables represented by the following words: ma, pop, pipe, peep, chip, chirp, cheese, she, bee, mutt, must, might, fright, thought, blink, and branch. The number and variety of acceptable syllables in English is bewildering. Hebrew syllables have much less variety than English syllables. In fact, Hebrew allows for only *two* kinds of syllables: open and closed. These are described below.

Open Syllables

Open syllables begin with a consonant that is followed by a vowel. That is as complicated as it gets.

Closed Syllables

Closed syllables begin with a consonant that is followed by a vowel and then closed off with a final consonant.

Notice that both open and closed syllables begin with a consonant. Thus, *every* syllable in Hebrew begins with a consonant. What differentiates open and closed syllables is the way they end.

Examples

מְדַבֵּר

By starting at the end of this word and working backwards toward the front, one can see that this word has two syllables. Because the last syllable ends with a consonant, the last syllable is a *closed* syllable (consonant-vowel-consonant). Thus, the last syllable is בֵּר. Still working backwards, the next consonant (ד) has a silent **Sheva** under it. (For guidelines on how to determine the difference between silent and vocal Shevas, see the

Appendix entitled Shevas in this resource.) The silent Sheva indicates that the ד has no vowel sound following it. The ד therefore is the last consonant in its syllable. Thus, this syllable, too, is *closed* and consists of מְד.

כֹּתֶב

By starting at the end of this word and working backwards toward the front, one can see that this word also has two syllables. Because the last syllable ends with a consonant, the last syllable must be *closed*. Thus, the last syllable is תֶב. Continuing to work backwards, the next symbol encountered is the long "o" vowel (Holem). That means this next syllable ends with a vowel and must therefore be an *open* syllable (consonant-vowel). This open syllable is כֹּ.

SHEVAS

The Sheva (pronounced she-**VAH**) appears as two vertical dots under a **consonant**. There are two kinds of Shevas (a vocal Sheva and a silent Sheva) and each one performs a different task. The differences between these two kinds of Shevas, as well as ways to tell them apart, are explained below.

Vocal Sheva

A vocal Sheva indicates a sound that hasn't risen to the level of a recognizable **vowel**. It is very short and usually sounds something like a brief grunt. In Hebrew (as in English), the vocal Sheva is what a normal vowel becomes when the accent shifts away from the **syllable** containing the vowel. In Hebrew, unlike English, the resulting change in sound that occurs from this accent shift is visually indicated by the spelling of the word.

Consider the following example in English, where such a change in pronunciation is not indicated. The last syllable of the word *photograph* has the short "a" sound. However, if the suffix -er is added to the word (*photographer*), the "a" no longer sounds like it did before. Even though in this English word the vowel is still written as an "a," it has become, in effect, a vocal Sheva.

In Hebrew, this change in pronunciation would be indicated by a change in the way the word is written. For example, the Hebrew word דָּבָר is pronounced *dah-VAHR*. That is, both syllables (*dah* and *VAHR*) contain the long "a" sound of the Qamets.

However, when the **masculine, plural** יִ ending is added to the word, the Qamets sound of the first syllable changes to the sound of a vocal Sheva — just as the "a" in *photograph* changed when the word changed to *photographer*. In Hebrew, however, this sound change is represented visually as well. So, with the masculine, plural ending added, דָּבָר becomes דְּבָרִים. Notice the vocal Sheva under the first consonant. For more information about how and when these vowel changes take place, see the Appendix in this resource entitled The Effect of Accents on Vowels.

Silent Sheva

A silent Sheva is almost always found under a consonant that is situated somewhere in the middle of a word. The only exception to this is the final Kaf, whose form includes a silent Sheva tucked up inside it (ךְ). A silent Sheva under a consonant indicates that the consonant is at the end of a syllable and so has no vowel sound immediately following it. For example, the Hebrew word מִדְבָּר has a silent Sheva under the ד. One would therefore read this word as *mid-BAHR*; that is, the ד (*d*) is at the end of the first syllable of the word and has no vowel sound immediately following it.

Because these two kinds of Shevas look identical but indicate different things, it is necessary to be able to tell them apart. Five ways to do this are described below.

How to Tell the Difference between a Silent and Vocal Sheva

1) When two Shevas occur together under two consecutive consonants, the first Sheva is a silent Sheva and the second Sheva is a vocal Sheva.

   For example, in the Hebrew word יִשְׁמְרוּ, the two Shevas occur side-by-side under the consecutive consonants שׁ and מ. So, the first Sheva is a silent Sheva and the second Sheva is a vocal Sheva. The word is therefore pronounced as *yish-mᵉ-ROO*. Note that the vocal Sheva is often indicated in English transliteration as a raised vowel in order to indicate its unusual and short sound.

2) After a preceding short vowel, the Sheva is a silent Sheva; after a preceding long vowel, the Sheva is a vocal Sheva.

   Consider, for example, the Hebrew word מִדְבָּר. The Sheva occurs after the short "i" vowel (Hireq). The Sheva under the ד is therefore a silent Sheva, which indicates that the ד is at the end of a syllable and so has no vowel sound immediately following it. So the word is pronounced *mid-BAHR*.

Now consider the Hebrew word כֹּתְבִים. The Sheva occurs after the long "o" vowel (Holem). The Sheva under the ת is therefore a vocal Sheva, which represents a brief grunt. So the word is pronounced *koh-tᵉ-VEEM*.

3) A Sheva beneath the first consonant of a word is a vocal Sheva.

For example, in the Hebrew word דְּבָרִים, the Sheva occurs under the ד, which is the first consonant of the word. The Sheva is therefore a vocal Sheva, and the word is pronounced *dᵉ-vah-REEM*.

4) A Sheva beneath a consonant containing a Dagesh Forte is a vocal Sheva.

For example, consider the Hebrew word דִּבְּרוּ. One might think that because the Sheva occurs after a short vowel (the short "i" — Hireq), the Sheva should be a silent Sheva (see #2 above). However, the ב has a Dagesh Forte inside it. (See the Appendix in this resource entitled Dageshes.) That means the word contains *two* בs — one ends a syllable and one begins the next syllable. The Sheva is therefore a vocal Sheva, and the word is pronounced *dib-bᵉ-ROO*.

5) A vocal Sheva cannot occur in a *closed* syllable. (For an explanation of closed and open syllables, see the Appendix in this resource entitled Syllables.)

Compound Shevas

One will also occasionally encounter in the Hebrew text a variation of the Sheva that looks like a combination of a Sheva and a short vowel. These have the technical name of Khatef (חָטֵף) vowels, but they are more commonly referred to as *reduced* vowels, *half*-vowels, or *compound* Shevas. There are three varieties of these vowels that are illustrated below under the consonant ע:

עֲ (Khatef Patakh—a very short "a" sound)

עֱ (Khatef Segol—a very short "e" sound)

עֳ (Khatef Qamets—a very short "o" sound)

When these vowels appear in the text, they will almost always be under one of the four **guttural** consonants. (See the Appendix entitled The Guttural Consonants in this resource.) These vowels are needed for guttural consonants instead of regular vocal Shevas because of the place where guttural consonants are formed. Because guttural consonants are formed back in the throat, they require extra air to be pronounced. The normal Sheva is insufficient to get the job done. When extra effort or air is expended to pronounce these more difficult consonants, the sound of the Sheva moves toward the sound of a short vowel. The resulting sound that falls between the grunt of a normal Sheva and the sound of a short vowel is indicated by the compound Sheva.

DAGESHES

The Dagesh appears as a dot in certain **consonant**s. There are two kinds of Dageshes and each kind performs a different task. The differences between these two kinds of Dageshes, as well as ways to tell them apart, are explained below.

Dagesh Forte

A Dagesh Forte (or Strong Dagesh) may appear as a dot in any consonant except the **guttural** consonants (א, ה, ח, and ע) and Resh (ר). The presence of the Dagesh Forte simply means that the consonant is doubled. In Hebrew, instead of writing the consonant twice, a Dagesh Forte is inserted in the consonant. So, for example, לֵּ is the equivalent of לְל.

Dagesh Lene

A Dagesh Lene (or Weak Dagesh) may only appear in six consonants: ב, ג, ד, כ, פ, and ת. (often called *BeGaDKeFaT* consonants—a made-up name consisting of these six consonants). The purpose of the Dagesh Lene was to distinguish between the two different sounds each one of these six consonants historically had. For example, with the Dagesh Lene, the Bet (ב) sounds like an English "b." Without the Dagesh Lene, the Bet (ב) sounds like an English "v." See **The Hebrew Consonants** for the different sounds these six consonants have (or historically had) with and without a Dagesh Lene.

How to Tell the Difference

An alert reader may have observed an area of overlap between the Dagesh Forte and the Dagesh Lene. If the Dagesh Forte can occur in ב, ג, ד, כ, פ, and ת, and the Dagesh Lene can also occur in these same consonants, then how does one tell whether a dot inside a ב, ג, ד, כ, פ, or ת is a Dagesh Forte or Dagesh Lene?

(Remember, only the *BeGaDKeFaT* consonants may have a Dagesh

Lene, so if you encounter a Dagesh in any other consonant, it is a Dagesh Forte and indicates that the consonant is doubled.)

For *BeGaDKeFaT* consonants, telling the Dageshes apart depends on whether or not the consonant is preceded by a vowel or a vocal Sheva. The following chart will help you to distinguish between the two Dageshes in every situation.

Is the Consonant Containing the Dagesh a *BeGaDKeFat* Consonant?

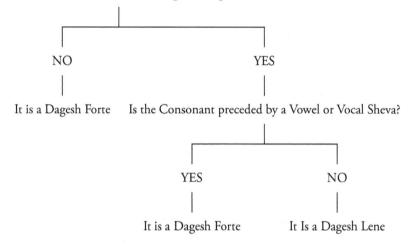

As can be seen in the above chart, the *only* time a dot inside a consonant can be a Dagesh Lene (instead of a Dagesh Forte) is when it occurs inside a *BeGaDKeFaT* letter that is not preceded by a vowel or a vocal Sheva.

THE EFFECT OF THE ACCENT ON VOWELS

Accents reflect the natural cadence of a language. They indicate where words and sentences place additional stress or force when pronounced. In English, as in Hebrew, accents can also determine how words are to be understood. Consider, for example, the difference in meaning between "permit" with the accent on the first **syllable** and "permit" with the accent on the last syllable. With the accent on the first syllable, the word is a **noun** meaning a written permission: "He received a building permit." With the accent on the second syllable, the word is a **verb** meaning "allow": "I do not permit you to go." Accents can also indicate the emphasis that accompanies surprise, a question, dismay, disgust, etc. Also, every language has a regular rhythm of pronunciation that is achieved by means of the expected accenting of particular words and places in sentences.

Their Form

In the printed Hebrew text, you can find an accent written above or below every word. They have a great variety of forms (see Gen 1:6 below). Every mark surrounding a word that is not a **vowel** sign, a circle (indicating a note in the side margin of BHS), or a lower case English letter (indicating a note at the bottom in the critical apparatus of BHS) is an accent mark. There are different forms of accents to indicate whether the accented word is associated with the following word (and if so, how closely) or if there is a pause between the accented word and the following word (and if so, how long a pause). Thus, accents in Hebrew perform many of the same functions that punctuation marks accomplish in English.

Accents and Vowels

An accent affects the length of the vowels of a word. That is, the kind and location of the accent determine whether the vowels of a word are long, short, or reduced (a **Sheva**). Accents that indicate a long pause after the word—corresponding to a period or comma in English—lengthen the vowel of the syllable on which they are placed. The two kinds of accents that regularly do this are the one that marks the end of a verse (the Silluq) and the one that marks the logical midpoint of the verse (the Atnakh). For example, consider Genesis 1:6, with all of its accents:

וַיֹּאמֶר אֱלֹהִים יְהִי רָקִיעַ בְּתוֹךְ הַמָּיִם וִיהִי מַבְדִּיל בֵּין מַיִם לָמָיִם:

"And God said, 'Let there be a vault between
the waters to separate water from water.'"

There are two thoughts in this verse: (1) the command for a vault between the waters, and (2) the purpose of the vault. The logical midpoint of the verse, then, is the junction between these two thoughts. That midpoint occurs in this case at the first occurrence of the word הַמָּיִם. The accent on this word is the Atnakh (the small, inverted, wishbone), and it has lengthened the short "a" vowel (Patakh) of the normal spelling of the word "waters" (מַיִם) to a long "a" vowel (Qamets).

This same lengthening of the "a" vowel occurs at the end of the verse. The accent on the last word is the Silluq (the small vertical line), and always occurs with the two vertical dots (Sof Pasuq) to mark the end of a verse. Again, the short "a" vowel (Patakh) of the normal spelling of the word "waters" (מַיִם) has been lengthened to a long "a" vowel (Qamets) because of this accent.

In addition to this regular vowel lengthening caused by the Atnakh and Silluq, accents of all kinds affect the vowels in every syllable of **noun**s and **adjective**s. How the vowels in a word's syllables are affected by the word's accent directly relates to the distance of the vowel from the accent. This relationship is indicated in the chart below:

	ACCENTED	NEXT TO ACCENT	FAR FROM ACCENT
OPEN SYLLABLE	long vowel	long vowel	Sheva
CLOSED SYLLABLE	long vowel	short vowel	short vowel

(It is important to remember that this chart applies only to the syllables in nouns and adjectives.)

To see how this chart works, consider, for example, the Hebrew **masculine, singular noun** דָּבָר It consists of two syllables: דָּ (an open syllable) and בָר (a closed syllable). (For an explanation of open and closed syllables, see the Appendix entitled Syllables in this resource.) The accent on Hebrew nouns and adjectives usually occurs on the last syllable. So, in this case, that last syllable is accented as expected and is also a closed syllable. According to the chart, a closed, accented syllable should have a long vowel—which it does. The first syllable of the word דָּבָר is an open syllable that is right next to the accented syllable. According to the chart, this kind of syllable should have a long vowel—which it does.

When the masculine, **plural** ending (ים) is added to the word, the accent moves to the new end of the word, and this affects the other vowels in the word. Following the guidelines described by the chart above, the vowel pattern of this masculine, plural noun is דְּבָרִים. The word now has three syllables: דְּ–בָ–רִים. The closed, accented syllable (רִים) has a long vowel; the open syllable next to the accent (בָ) has a long vowel; and the open syllable far from the accent (דְּ) has a Sheva.

The rules outlined above generally apply to all Hebrew nouns and adjectives and describe the language's natural cadence represented by its system of accents. However, some vowels are unaffected by the movement of the accent. These unchangeable vowels include vowels that are written in conjunction with a consonantal form (for example, וֹ, וּ, and י). When, according to the chart, the syllable containing these vowels should have a Sheva, the vowel in the syllable next to the accent may reduce to a Sheva instead.

— HOW TO PRONOUNCE — HEBREW WORDS

Hebrew was originally written using only **consonant**s. When the symbols for **vowel**s were later added, those symbols had to be fit in wherever there was room. The Hebrew vowel symbols or signs are therefore written above, below, and around the consonants. For the sounds of the Hebrew consonants and vowels, and the effect on pronunciation caused by **Dageshes** and **Shevas**, see the corresponding Appendices in this resource. Pronouncing Hebrew words is essentially combining the information in these Appendices.

Figuring out how to pronounce Hebrew words is greatly facilitated by the fact that every Hebrew **syllable** must begin with a consonant followed by a vowel or a vocal Sheva. We therefore begin at the right end of the Hebrew word and read right-to-left, alternating between consonants and vowels. When we come to a consonant that is *not* followed by a vowel, then we complete the pronunciation of that syllable with that consonant and then resume our consonant-vowel alternation beginning with the next syllable. The accent tells us where to put the emphasis on the spoken word. A couple of examples should make this process clear. The first example is the first form in the Hebrew Bible (Gen 1:1):

$$\text{בְּרֵאשִׁית}$$

We begin pronouncing this word by pronouncing the first consonant (בּ) and its following vocal Sheva. We know that the following ר, cannot be a part of this first syllable because the ר is followed by its own vowel (Tsere). Thus, the first syllable is read from top to bottom, and is pronounced *bᵉ*:

$$\text{בְּ↓}$$

The next syllable begins with a ר, which is followed by a Tsere. The following א has no vowel under, over, or after it, so it must be a part of this syllable as well. Thus, reading this syllable from top to bottom and right to left, we pronounce it as *ray*:

The last syllable begins with a שׁ, which is followed by a Hireq Yod. The following ת has no vowel under, over, or after it, so it must be a part of this syllable as well. Thus, reading this syllable from top to bottom and right to left, we pronounce it as *sheet*:

שִׁית

Notice that this last syllable is also the accented syllable. The entire word, therefore, would be pronounced as *bᵉ-ray-SHEET.*

For the next example, consider the first form in Genesis 8:1:

וַיִּזְכֹּר

Once again, we begin at the right and work our way left to the end of the word. We begin with the consonant ו, followed by a Patakh. We notice that the next consonant (י) has a Dagesh Forte inside of it. That means the consonant is doubled. Since a doubled consonant may never end (or begin) a syllable in Hebrew, one י must end the first syllable and the second י must begin the next syllable. So, reading from top to bottom and right to left, the first syllable is pronounced *vigh* (the Patakh and the Yod combine to form the sound of a long "i" in English).

וַי

The second syllable consists of the second י, followed by the Hireq. The next consonant, the ז, does not have any vowel following it (a silent Sheva signals no vowel) and so must be a part of this syllable as well. Thus, reading this syllable from top to bottom and right to left, we pronounce it as *yiz*:

נֹ֖ר

The third and last syllable begins with a כ, is followed by a Holem, and ends with a ר. Thus, reading this syllable from right to left, we pronounce it as *kohr*:

כֹּ֖ר
←

Notice that this last syllable is also the accented syllable. The entire word, therefore, would be pronounced as *vigh-yiz-KOHR*.

With practice, pronouncing Hebrew words will become much easier and enable you to confidently share with others the findings of your computer-assisted exegesis.

SCRIPTURE INDEX

— SELECT BIBLIOGRAPHY —
FOR FURTHER STUDY

For those readers whose interest in biblical Hebrew has been awakened and would therefore like to explore the details of the language in a little more depth, the following resources are suggested as appropriate for the beginning student.

Beginning Hebrew Grammars

Futato, Mark D. *Beginning Biblical Hebrew*. Winona Lake, IN: Eisenbrauns, 2003.

Pratico, Gary D. and Van Pelt, Miles V. *Basics of Biblical Hebrew*. Grand Rapids: Zondervan, 2007.

Ross, Allen P. *Introducing Biblical Hebrew*. Grand Rapids: Baker Academic, 2001.

Grammatical Helps

Long, Gary A. *Grammatical Concepts 101 for Biblical Hebrew: Learning Biblical Hebrew Grammatical Concepts through English Grammar*. Peabody, MA: Hendrickson, 2002.

Van Pelt, Miles V. *English Grammar to Ace Biblical Hebrew*. Grand Rapids: Zondervan, 2010.

Hebrew Text Resources

Elliger, K. and W. Rudolph eds. *Biblia Hebraica Stuttgartensia*. 5th ed. Stuttgart: Deutsche Bibelgesellschaft, 1997.

Scott, William R. *A Simplified Guide to BHS*. Berkeley, CA: Bibal Press, 1987.

Leading Bible Software Resources

Accordance Bible Software. Developed by OakTree Software, Inc. (www.accordancebible.com).

BibleWorks. Developed by BibleWorks LLC (www.bibleworks.com).

Logos Bible Software. Developed by Logos Research Systems, Inc. (www.logos.com).

Olive Tree Bible Software. A division of HarperCollins Christian Publishing. (www.OliveTree.com).

Printed in the USA
CPSIA information can be obtained
at www.ICGtesting.com
LVHW020709050824
787165LV00009B/66

9 780310 521303